W9-BAW-246

A Divine Invitation

Steve McVey

HARVEST HOUSE™ PUBLISHERS

EUGENE, OREGON

Cover by Left Coast Design, Portland, Oregon

A DIVINE INVITATION
Copyright © 2002 by Steve McVey
Published by Harvest House Publishers
Eugene, Oregon 97402

Library of Congress Cataloging-in-Publication Data
McVey, Steve, 1954–
   A divine invitation / Steve McVey
   ISBN 0-7369-0849-8
 1. Christian Life. I. Title.
  BV4501.3 .M39 2002
  248.4—dc21   2002023299

Printed in the United States of America.

05 06 07 08 09 10 11 / VP-CF / 10 9 8 7 6 5 4 3

To Hannah, Jonathan, and Jeremy

May you forever delight
in God's intimate embrace.

Acknowledgments

Authors don't write books in a vacuum. Ideas are planted, take root, grow, and finally yield fruit as God uses people and circumstances in the writer's life. *A Divine Invitation* comes to fruition after numerous friends have made contributions for which I am deeply grateful.

My gratitude goes to Cheryl Buchanan, Tim and Debbie Childers, Steve Drake, Tom Grady, Barry Grecu, Brenda Josee, Bob and Sheree Lykens, John Nil, Judy Reamer, John Rivenbark, Glenna Salsbury, and Fred Schueller—all of whom advised, contributed personal stories, and encouraged me in various ways throughout the writing process.

Particular thanks are in order for Anthony and Beth Ross, whose generosity in providing a cabin retreat at a pivotal time in my life provided an environment in which I could hear my Divine Lover's voice whispering to me in an unmistakable way.

I am indebted to my editor, Nick Harrison, for his interest, encouragement, and advice on this book. Nick is a kindred spirit whose spiritual paradigm is very much like my own.

Bob Hawkins, Jr. and the whole staff at Harvest House Publishers deserve much credit for any book I write. Their hard work, professionalism, and zeal are obvious witnesses to the fact that publishing books isn't just a job but a ministry to them.

I will always be grateful for the writings of Brennan Manning. I've read and assimilated so much of what he has written that I'm not sure anymore what I learned from his books and what God taught me from elsewhere. The Holy Spirit has used his writings to teach me more about my Abba's love than I had ever known.

Other than Jesus Christ, Himself, my deepest appreciation in life is for my precious wife, Melanie. In every way, she is everything that any man could hope for in a wife. Since we first met in 1970, she has been my greatest encourager and friend.

May Jesus Christ be glorified and His beauty and love be revealed to every person who reads this book. He, above all, deserves both gratitude and glory forever.

Contents

Foreword

The love of our great God and Savior has been a driving motivation in my life from the day I first met Him. I first encountered this incredible love as a young businessman who had dedicated his life to amassing wealth and living a life of comfort. As I grew in the knowledge of just how great and deep His love actually is, I began to grow in a desire to share it with others as well.

In 1951, 24 hours after my precious wife Vonette and I decided to sign a contract to become His slaves, God gave me a vision for what now is Campus Crusade for Christ, a ministry dedicated to spreading His love all over the world. He has mightily blessed this vision, and now, with thousands of staff members and trained volunteers, we have preached the Good News in every country on earth. My joy has increased daily as I have seen many come to realize God's love, given to us completely through His Son, Jesus, and His ultimate act of love on the cross.

And yet, in the midst of my joy, I am saddened as I realize that many Christians who have tasted God's love remain ignorant of how powerful, passionate, and all-encompassing it truly is. Having received forgiveness for their sins, they often turn to a life of self-effort, hoping their forced acts of devotion and religious activities will cause God to continue loving them, not knowing that His love is already theirs in its incredible entirety. Then, all they feel is frustration, emptiness, and a growing sense of disillusion-ment. They may even conclude that the love they experienced was nothing more than a desperate fig-ment of their imagination.

For those Christians, and for all others, I strongly rec-ommend this book. Steve McVey has given us, in very clear and understandable language, a wonderful, indelible picture of just how beautiful, complete, and even startling

God's love for us really is. Steve is excited by it, and he makes us excited along with him. This is only natural, considering the subject—our Lord's passion for mankind, which if fully comprehended, would make every person who ever lived fall to his or her knees in astonishment.

Steve also shows how laughable we are to ever think there is anything we could do to earn it or retain it or think we have lost it. Hurting believers everywhere would experience healing and renewal if they would internalize the message of this book.

Take these stirring words to heart. God is waiting to speak to you, and your life will be changed. That's what His love does.

Bill Bright
Founder and Chairman
Campus Crusade for Christ

1

Too Busy for Love

IN A CABIN BESIDE A POND IN southern Georgia, God started something that would ultimately turn my world upside down—or to be more precise, right side up. I had come to this country setting primarily to speak at a conference, but I arrived four days ahead of schedule so that I could catch up on some long-overdue work. My major goals were to complete a magazine article I had been asked to write and to get some solid work done on my next book, whose deadline crunch I was feeling more and more.

Yet as I sat down to write, something seemed wrong. I couldn't get started. My thoughts were deadlocked. For hours I tried to buckle down and get to work, but to no avail.

"What's going on, Lord?" I finally asked. "You know that I've set aside this time to write."

Someone has rightly said that if you want to give God a good laugh, tell Him *your* plans. I'm sure I must have made Him snicker that day.

Then, in answer to my question, I heard God speak. It wasn't an audible voice, but it was a thought that came into my mind that I knew was from Him. "That's not *My* plan for you being here," I heard Him say. And that was that. I spent most of my time for the four days sitting alone in complete solitude and silence. Although the rural setting was beautiful, the days there were *long* days.

It's hard for me to be still very long. I love being busy. When I go on vacation, it usually takes me a few days just to settle down and arrive emotionally and mentally at our destination. Even at home, I find it hard to sit still and do nothing. Sometimes my wife, Melanie, will watch me pacing from the computer to the television to the couch and back to the computer and will finally say, "Will you perch somewhere?"

I thrive on activity. People often applaud that kind of attitude. Folks like me are seldom called lazy. "Driven," yes. "Insensitive," sometimes. "Impatient," often. But one thing is sure: we get things done whether they need to get done or not.

Sitting alone one evening in the country cabin, I began to read an article from a magazine someone had left there. The author was recounting a scene from the movie *Coal Miner's Daughter*. She described a scene in which Loretta Lynn is on stage—a Loretta who did way too much, too soon, too fast. On the verge of a breakdown and wiping at a free fall of tears, she told her beloved fans, "Patsy Cline used to tell me, 'Little gal—you got to run your own life!' But I can tell you, my friends, right now, my life's a-runnin' me."[1]

As I read the article, my emotions were stirred. At the same time, I found it mildly amusing that God seemed to be speaking to me through the words of Patsy Cline and Loretta Lynn. (I've never been a big fan of country music.) *My life's a-runnin' me.* The words echoed in my mind all night.

Less than four years earlier, I had established a ministry that focuses on teaching Christians about their identity in Christ and about resting in Him, allowing Him to literally live His life through each individual believer. From the outset, ministry opportunities had been phenomenal. As a result of the success of my first book, *Grace Walk*, an avalanche of speaking invitations had come, allowing me the opportunity to travel all over the world. I never thought for a moment that it was because of me, or even the book, that the opportunities were abundant. I saw it as a sovereign work of God, a decision He made to launch me into ministry in a way I had never imagined.

I have preached in a leper colony in India; in illegal, underground house churches in China; in bullfighting rings and downtown plazas in Mexico. The invitations have poured in from across North America, Asia, Europe, Africa, and Latin America. I often tell my friends that I have felt like a child in a candy store with unlimited access to the inventory. My life seemed to be on cruise control with nothing ahead except more opportunities to do what I love doing.

Then one morning something happened that seemed insignificant at the time. I woke up with an itchy scalp caused by a rash. After a few days, it went away, and I thought no more about it. A short time later the same kind of rash showed up on my ankle. It went away too, only to show up another time on my calf. After seeing this burning irritant reappear this many times, I finally went to the doctor. He took one look at it and said, "Tell me about your lifestyle."

"What do you mean?" I asked.

"Is your work stressful?" he asked.

"I love what I do," I responded rather defensively.

"That doesn't mean it isn't stressful," he answered. Then my doctor proceeded to announce that this persistent rash was the result of nothing other than stress. *Stress?* Not a good diagnosis for a man who teaches others how to rest in Christ. The doctor recommended I slow down, so I left his office thinking that I'd try to take it a little easier.

Intimacy Interrupted

As I sat alone in my rural resort where God had led me, He began to show me some things about my lifestyle that were painful to admit. I began to realize that I had unknowingly fallen back into some of the same patterns of self-sufficient living I had experienced when I was a pastor who didn't understand his identity in Christ. I had been living as if everything rises and falls on measurable results. How many conferences could I lead in a year? How many Grace Walk Ministries offices could we establish? How many foreign countries could I visit during the next twelve months? How much can I do? My motives were admirable, but my driven approach to life and ministry had set off an alarm through my unwelcome rash.

God had already allowed me to face some not-so-subtle clues that something had jumped the track in my daily life. One day I was driving down the interstate, when somebody in the lane beside me suddenly cut in front of me. Instead of hitting the brake, I reached for the gearshift and almost put the car in park without thinking. Then there were the numerous times I walked into the office of my Administrative Manager, Cheryl, to tell her something, only to discover that I couldn't remember what I came to tell her. There were many incidents like that. One morning I stood at the bathroom sink asking myself, "Did I brush my teeth yet?"

In an effort to organize my thoughts and document my response to what God was showing me during my cabin encounter with Him, I opened my laptop and wrote the following words.

I feel like Lucy Ricardo working on the production line at the candy factory. I can't keep up, and I can't swallow any more. What is God showing me to do? I believe that He is redirecting my life and ministry, leading me to focus on the things He has called me to and reminding me to not become distracted by lesser, albeit good, things. I need to remember that *bigger* is not necessarily *better*, that to be busier isn't necessarily to be more productive. I need to learn that I don't have to say yes to every "great opportunity" that comes along.

I want to grow in my knowledge of God and His ways. I want to experience greater intimacy with Him. I want to be obsessed with Him, so that the things that don't matter *won't* matter. I want to be inwardly at rest. I want my mind to stop whirling all the time with thoughts, plans, and ideas. I want to be able to relax mentally and to feel an emotional calmness by default. I want to cry with joy over God's manifest presence.

Reading the words I had written, my problem became clear to me. I was hungry to experience deeper intimacy with Jesus Christ, but had become distracted by my hyperactive lifestyle. I had allowed the mechanics of ministry and "living a Christian life" to rob me of the exhilarating awareness of the indwelling presence of Christ. The enemy had used his classic weapon against me—enticing me to focus more on "the Christian life" than on Christ Himself. I sincerely loved the Lord, but had temporarily lost that sense of intimate union known only by those who are *in love* with Jesus.

Can you relate to my dilemma? The specifics of our circumstances are probably different, but most of us in the modern church face this same basic temptation: allowing ourselves to become so busy with life that we miss the promised abundance of *the Life* that God has given us.

(See John 10:10.) God has chosen you to be His bride for a specific reason—He wants to pour out His love on us. He wants to pour out His love on *you*.

A Covert Attack

Jesus said in John 17:3 that the meaning of eternal life revolves around *knowing* God. The word is the same one used by the mother of Jesus when she questioned the angelic announcement of Jesus' birth by saying, "How can this be, since I *know* no man?" The word denotes experiential intimacy with someone. God saved you because He wants to *know* you. He is consumed with a resolve to love you like you've never been loved before, with an intensity and commitment greater than you can possibly imagine. Meanwhile, in the modern church, most of us don't have time for love-making. There are too many other things that need to be done.

Since God's greatest desire toward His bride is to love us with a love that is divine, it makes sense that our adversary's greatest mission is to prevent us from experiencing that love. If a frontal attack from the enemy can't make us turn away from Jesus Christ by seducing us back to the world, he will utilize another battle plan. He will cause us to become preoccupied with everything else—in fact, with *anything* other than Jesus Christ.

Many believers have been taken prisoners of war through a covert attack from hell, and sadly, they don't even know it. They are being held captive in a prison of *busyness*. They sincerely desire to advance spiritually and often wonder why they aren't making more progress. But there is a reason they walk in circles: that's all anybody in a prison cell *can* do.

Author Richard Foster has said that in contemporary culture, our adversary majors in three things: noise, hurry, and crowds. While it might be argued that there is nothing inherently wrong with any of these three, it is possible for them to become enemies of our spiritual well-being. When we become so busy with our lifestyle that we forfeit the consciousness of who Jesus is in us and who we are in Him, we have unwittingly been taken prisoner.

The ongoing awareness of His indwelling life in us isn't a legalistic discipline that we grit our teeth and determine to practice. It is an underlying state of *abiding in Christ* at all times. To abide in Him is to assume a continuous posture of total dependence on Christ as the source of our life at every moment and in every situation. It is the default setting of one who is living out of the union he shares with God through Jesus Christ.

Quaker missionary Thomas Kelly wrote in his classic book, *A Testament of Devotion,*

> There is a way of ordering our mental life on more than one level at once. On one level we may be thinking, discussing, seeing, calculating, meeting all the demands of external affairs. But deep within, behind the scenes, at a profounder level, we may also be in prayer and adoration, song and worship and a gentle receptiveness to divine breathings.[2]

Kelly describes the condition experienced by people when they first become Christians. Do you remember when you first became a believer how *enamored* you were with Jesus Christ? Even when you weren't consciously thinking about Him, the reality of His presence rested just beneath your conscious thoughts. For the first time, you were aware that He was there inside you, loving you in a way you had never known until then. With the slightest provocation, you would find yourself whispering a prayer, witnessing to a friend, thinking of Jesus and what He meant to you. You were present to Him and He to you at every moment. As Kelly noted, you had "a gentle receptiveness to divine breathings."

Many who once knew the reality of that kind of faith have lost it. They didn't lose it through an act of defiance. Instead it was lost through an attitude of *duty*. They became so preoccupied with duties at home, at work, and at church that somehow the love affair they once enjoyed with Jesus simply faded. Ask these people today if they love the Lord, and without hesitation they will affirm that they do. Ask them if they are experiencing the kind of intimate relationship with Jesus they once knew, and they will be forced to admit that things have changed.

They aren't unlike the young mom who responded to her husband's complaint that she never wanted to make love to him anymore with the admission, "I'm just too tired." It isn't because most Christians don't love Jesus that they have lost their sense of intimacy with Him. It's just that they have become focused on so many other things that they simply don't have any energy left for Him. When is the last time you sat alone in silence and pondered on how *much* you are loved by God? How many hundreds of acts of "Christian service" have you done since that last time?

Service Without Love

"So what's wrong with the fact that I've been busy with my Christian duties?" one may ask. The Apostle Paul answers: "If I have the gift of prophecy, and know all mysteries and all knowledge; and if I have all faith, so as to remove mountains, but do not have love, I am nothing. And if I give all my possessions to feed the poor, and if I surrender my body to be burned, but do not have love, it profits me nothing" (1 Corinthians 13:2-3). So much for "Christian service" separated from a love relationship.

In the chapters that follow I want to present to you a certain kind of love. It's a love that's different from anything I understood for many years—a love different from anything most people have ever known. It would be impossible to explain it, so I'm simply going to try to describe it to you.

Its depth and breadth extend far beyond the bounds of human reasoning. To the unenlightened eye, it would seem to be irrational, maybe even eccentric. Within the narrow confines of ordinary common sense, this kind of love makes *no* sense. Its object is so undeserving. Its Source is so unfathomable. And the medium of its expression suggests a sort of divine absurdity that defies anything understood by men and women.

The conduit through which this love flows is a cross— a barbaric tool of revenge that for millennia has epitomized the greatest agony and the deepest shame one may know. Historically, the cross was reserved for the vilest of the human race. It was considered to be the place where the trash of the universe finally met the incinerator of justice. It was here that the baby-killer finally identified with the horror he had inflicted on pure innocence. It was at this place that the calloused and obstinate criminal would finally weep like a small schoolgirl. It was where the worst possible offenders would finally be joined with the worst possible consequence. It was on this bloody altar that agony and agape met and embraced. Since that day, nothing has been the same.

Our relationship with God exists, not because we one day decided to "do the Christian thing," but because God sovereignly chose us, then set all of His divine resources in motion to bring to pass what He determined to accomplish in us (see Romans 8:29-30). The cross changed everything for you. When, by the death of Jesus Christ on the cross, divine love satisfied the demands of divine justice, you became the beneficiary. When Jesus cried out "It is finished!" from the cross, He declared that believers owe God nothing.

"Are you suggesting that we owe God *nothing* at all, even after all that He has done for us?" one pastor asked me.

"Kurt, what *could* you owe God for all that He has done for you?" I asked. "How could we ever repay God for a priceless gift?"

"Of course, I know we could never repay Him," Kurt said. "But we can spend our lives *trying* to repay Him."

"And *how* do we do that?" I persisted. "What could we offer God that would even *begin* to repay Him for His goodness to us?" Kurt's perspective isn't an uncommon one, but my question to him begs an answer. How could we ever repay God for His great gift of eternal life in Jesus Christ?

Adam and Joshua were best friends who served in Vietnam together, often fighting side by side during intense battles. One day Adam's unit pulled out, and he was stuck alone behind the enemy line. He had been wounded and wasn't able to stand to his feet. Upon discovering what had happened, Joshua rushed back into the heat of the conflict and battled his way to the foxhole where Adam lay without hope. Joshua threw his friend across his shoulders and began to run for safety. As he approached the protection of his own unit, Joshua was shot in the back. He collapsed forward into another foxhole where his allies immediately cared for both him and Adam.

Joshua spent a month in the hospital, requiring back surgery and physical therapy. He had paid a great price to save his buddy. But to him, Adam was worth it. After all, they were best friends.

One day after they arrived back home, Joshua came home to find Adam putting his lawn mower back into his garage. "What are you doing?" Joshua asked.

"I just came over and mowed your lawn," Adam answered.

"Why?" Joshua asked.

"Well, I was thinking about it," Adam said. "You saved my life in 'Nam, and I thought maybe I could try to repay you by mowing your lawn."

How do you think Joshua felt when Adam told him that? I confess that this event didn't really happen. I simply tell it to illustrate the folly of using insignificant gestures to repay someone who has sacrificed greatly on our behalf. For Adam to think he could begin to repay Joshua by mowing his lawn would be absurd. Worse than that, it would be an insult to Joshua, who had risked his life for his friend. Joshua didn't save Adam's life to get his lawn mowed. He saved him because he loved his friend.

We are all born sons and daughters of Adam, destined for destruction—yet believers have been rescued by our Joshua—Jesus Christ. He didn't simply *risk* His life. He *gave* His life for us. What could we ever do to repay Him? There is nothing that we *can* do, but to accept the fact that He loves us that much. Will His love make a difference in how we act? Of course it will! However, our behavior is the result of His actions toward us, not a repayment for them. Don't try to pay a price for a priceless gift. To do so only demonstrates that we have no concept of the gift's infinite value. Worse yet, it is an insult to the One who gave the gift.

The word "gospel" means "good news." And here's the best part of the good news—you don't have to try to repay God. To do so is to attempt to enter into some kind of mercenary relationship to Him, and that is not at all what He has on His mind! God's desire is that you will grow in your knowledge of His love and your capacity to receive it. Forget what you think you owe Him and accept, by faith, that it has already been paid.

Imagine a particular kind of life for a moment. It's a life in which God requires nothing from you. In this life, His purpose is not that you should try to give Him anything. He, on the other hand, intends to give you everything necessary for your complete fulfillment. In this life, there is nothing you could ever do that would cause God to love you any more or any less than He does right now. *Imagine that nothing you do could ever change how God feels about you in even the slightest degree.* Think of Him loving you with a passionate, unconditional love that will never end.

This life is not an imaginary one, but a real one. As His bride, you are one about whom He has dreamed for all eternity. The hopes and plans of Deity rest within you. Even if your past religious indoctrination or your sense of spiritual inadequacy causes your mind to resist such a life as the one I've described, something deep within your spirit may resonate with this description of the life God wants you to live every day. Thomas Kelly describes it this way:

> Deep within us all there is an amazing inner sanctuary of the soul, a holy place, a Divine Center, a speaking Voice, to which we may continually return. Eternity is in our hearts, pressing upon our time-torn lives, warming us with intimations of an astounding destiny, calling us home unto Itself. Yielding to these persuasions, gladly committing ourselves in body and soul, utterly and completely, to the Light Within, is the beginning of true life.[3]

I don't believe that my experience as I have described it is unique. I served as a local church pastor for more than 20 years, and since resigning the pastorate in 1994, I have traveled many miles and spoken in many churches. I find that intimacy between Christ and Christians is often conspicuously absent in modern church life. Many of us are dutifully doing the disciplines we believe are indispensable to our faith, but we have lost the wonder of it all. We have lost the experience of sharing passionate love with the One who gave Himself for us so that we might enjoy that very intimacy.

For years I prayed, asking the Lord to help me to love Him more. As I have grown spiritually, I have come to realize that the only way we can grow in our love for Him is to grow in the knowledge of His love for us. "We love, because He first loved us" (1 John 4:19). God's love for us through Jesus Christ is the source of our love response toward Him.

Do you long for a more intimate walk with God? Is there a yearning deep within you to experience a conscious intimacy with Him that runs deeper than every other experience of life? Your very desire for God is an act of His grace operating in you. Sadly, many people have no such hunger for God. If you have any doubt about your own hunger, the question must be raised as to why you would even be reading this book. You *do* hunger for Him. What then makes you so different? It isn't because of some intrinsic virtue within us that we hunger for God. It's because He has miraculously placed that hunger there so that He can then satisfy it. In other words, your hunger to know God intimately is proof that He is working in your life, and make no mistake about it, God will finish what He starts. "For I am confident of this very thing, that He who began a good work in you will perfect it until the day of Christ Jesus" (Philippians 1:6).

It is my prayer that the chapters that follow will cause you to see God's love from a perspective and to an extent that you may not have seen it before. As you read the pages that follow, be mindful of the fact that no description of God's love for the Christian can be exaggerated. To the contrary, "[His] lovingkindness is great to the heavens and [His] truth to the clouds" (Psalm 57:10). "I love you *this much!*" God says to you as He stretches out His arms across the clouds.

God's infinite love can never be fully described using finite words, but the Holy Spirit can speak to us beyond the medium of words. It is my prayer that God will say more to you than this book can possibly say. You may find it helpful in progressing through these pages to put aside your preconceived ideas about God's love and imagine that you are a blank page, waiting for His Spirit to write a love letter in your heart. However big you imagine God's love for you to be, it is bigger. Open your heart and mind now to receive what He wants to reveal and say to you. Allow the reading of these pages to be not only an exercise of the mind, but a journey of the heart. Be open to the possibility of having both your thoughts *and* emotions stimulated by the Holy Spirit. May your God-given faith and hunger lovingly push you toward a greater awareness of His passion for you until you are love struck in such a way that you never get over it—not for all eternity.

Walking Together

Let's walk together with the Holy Spirit as we learn more of the depths of His love. Cooperate with God at each step where He reveals truth to you and works in your life. If the prayers at the end of each chapter express your heart, then affirm to God that they reflect your thoughts and desires. Pause before beginning the next chapter and interact with your Heavenly Father. Take time to let God make the truth of His love real.

Dear Father,

I have often become so busy in the details of my daily living that I have missed the joy of the love relationship You want to have with me. Open my mind and heart to discover the truths You want me to know. Reveal your love to me so that I understand and experience it in new and greater ways. Speak to me, dear Holy Spirit. I am listening.

G.R.A.C.E. GROUP QUESTIONS

A G.R.A.C.E. (Giving & Receiving Affirmative Christian Encouragement) Group is any gathering of people who meet together to encourage and strengthen each other in the grace of God. Use the discussion questions at the end of each chapter to facilitate further learning and discussion. The truths of this book will be worked further into your life as you consider these questions. If you're not a member of a G.R.A.C.E. group, answer the questions on your own by writing a brief response to each one.

1. Describe the last time you heard God speak to you. Discuss some of the various ways in which God may speak today. Identify at least three different ways that God spoke in the Bible.

2. What are some of the distractions in modern church life which actually may interfere with intimacy with Jesus Christ? What is the one thing in your life that is most likely to interfere with your own sense of intimacy with God?

3. What is your favorite verse in the Bible which speaks about God's love? Discuss how Romans 8:29-30 relates to the love God has for those who are in Him.

4. How would you define the meaning of intimacy with God? Describe the lifestyle of a Christian who is experiencing intimacy with Him.

2
Forgiven and Forgotten

RECENTLY SOMEONE TOLD ME A STORY that for many years of my life would have been very hard for me to accept because it contradicts much of what I had always believed. John (I'll change his name to protect the guilty) and his wife, Sarah, were taking a trip in a foreign country. John had professed knowing the Lord for a long time and had even told his friends that he believed God was going to use his life in a big way.

One day John and Sarah found themselves in a certain city at a place where they never should have gone, a place where they *wouldn't* have gone if they had been trusting in God at the moment. In some ways, what they did wasn't unique. Certainly, they aren't the only people who have ever been to some places and done some things they shouldn't have.

However, in this instance John soon found himself in over his head. Sarah was a good-looking woman, and they weren't exactly in an environment where the fact that they were married mattered to anybody. He looked around and saw tough, crude, strong men there, the kind that often frequent sleazy back street bars in the bad part of town. It occurred to John that these characters wouldn't hesitate to do whatever they had to do to him for the chance to get at his wife. So John did the unthinkable—he told Sarah to do whatever the men asked. Maybe by doing what they wanted, the two of them could get out of this situation still alive.

Circumstances unfolded exactly as John had feared. My friend who told me this story said that John actually let his wife go home with one of these men, while he waited there for her to return. What is even more difficult to believe is that after this situation happened, John continued on with his trip, still professing to love God and claiming to have a desire to follow Him. Some might say he couldn't really be a believer and act that way, but John is a minister who is considered by many people to be a great spiritual leader.

What are your thoughts about this man? Is there any way that he could indeed be a spiritual leader? I might add that what he did didn't stay hidden. Eventually, everybody found out about it. Everyone who knows about him also knows about this incident. It's also noteworthy that this sin didn't happen before he came to the Lord. It happened afterwards, while he was professing to follow God's guidance for his life.

I encourage you to pause in your reading for a moment and identify in your own mind what you believe about this man's circumstances. Can God use him in ministry to others, or did his actions permanently disqualify him from being used by God? Would you take spiritual advice from him? What would you say about the likelihood that God would ever use this man's life? Would it make any difference to you if I told you that later, on another occasion, he used the same trickery to protect himself from *another* man? It's true—he did! Knowing that, what do you think are his chances of being somebody who can ever have spiritual impact on others?

The People God Uses

Allow me to explain the missing details of this incident. The Friend who told me the story about this man is the Holy Spirit. He told this story in the Bible in Genesis 12. As I relayed the story to you I called the man John, but his real name is Abraham. The story is about how he and Sarah traveled to Egypt and committed this sin while they were there.

It's an amazing (and sometimes confusing) aspect of God's grace that He will indeed use a man like Abraham. Not only was he used by God, but in Hebrews 11, as if He has completely forgotten that He already gave us the low-down on this man in Genesis, the Holy Spirit lists Abraham as a *hero* of our faith. Most people wouldn't even recommend Abraham as "Husband of the Year," but God lists him as a man of great faith. Apparently there is something about the way God judges people that is very different from the way most of us view others or ourselves. He looks *past* behavior and into the heart more readily than we can even imagine.

The application of this message is scary to many Christians. They're afraid that this kind of illustration will encourage sin in people's lives, but in reality most people don't need encouragement in order to sin. There is already an abundance of encouragement to sin in the world around us. If anybody decides to sin, including the Christian, we don't need encouragement to do it. People will sin with or without it.

When, as new Christians, we move from the world into the church, there is much encouragement about how *not* to sin. One young Christian said, "The Christians at the church where I grew up sure weren't interested in intimacy or spiritual growth. They were just interested in not drinking."[1] Most of us have been given list upon list of suggestions about how to keep from sinning. On the one hand, the world encourages us to sin. On the other, the church encourages us *not* to sin. However, I don't find much encouragement anywhere for those who *have* sinned—which includes all of us. Don't think you haven't sinned just because your misdeeds don't fall into the same category as Abraham's sin. Adultery is a horrible sin, but as a local church pastor for more than 20 years, I saw a great deal of damage done in the church by gossip and murmuring. Adultery is sin—but so is gossip. It's easy to identify the "hall of shame" sins in the lives of others and yet be blind to the insidious sins in our own life.

There will always be those who sit in condescending judgment on the ones who have miserably failed. They are like the elder brother in the story of the prodigal son. They sneer at those who have foolishly sinned despite the fact that they are just as miserable after their faithful service as the "sinner" is after his folly. Licentiousness and legalism are two sides of the same performance-based coin. They both produce the same dryness of soul that cries out for the miraculous outpouring of God's thirst-quenching grace.

This chapter is not directed to those who are held captive by the most serious sin—that of not seeing their own sins. Instead, it's my prayer that the Holy Spirit will give comfort and encouragement to Christians who *know* they have sinned. To such people, God's message is that His love for you is greater than your sins—far greater. Even if you have sinned in a big way, "where sin is big, God's grace is bigger" (See Romans 5:20)! I'll say it so plainly that it may sound shocking to a legalistic mind—*you cannot out-sin the love of God!*

Don't misunderstand. It's not my intent to minimize the seriousness of sin. Sin is a serious matter. It was for our sin that Christ went to the cross. However, this chapter is addressed to those who have sinned and know it. It's written with the hope that the Holy Spirit will release those who are conscious of their sins from self-condemnation and feelings of spiritual inferiority. Many believers have never enjoyed true intimacy with God because they are continually held in bondage by shame over their past sins. My intention here is not to be soft on sin, but to be soft on people who are hurting from sin!

Having put to rest the fears of those who are afraid that undiluted grace may encourage sin, let's turn our attention to *you*, the one who has sinned and knows it. Jesus said that those who are well have no need for a doctor, and that He can't help them. But those who know that they have been infected by sin and need help are the ones whom He seeks. If you are like the overwhelming majority of Christians, you can point to incidents in your own past, or perhaps even in your present behavior, that make you feel ashamed. Know this: you are in good company.

An Unlikely Hall of Fame

Hebrews 11 lists those people whom God considers role models for the community of faith. A quick glance at the names mentioned there might lead one to conclude that God isn't very picky about whom He is willing to use. If the modern church were to form such a list, we probably wouldn't have included many of those mentioned in that chapter. Or, if we had decided to list their names, at least we would have left out some of the gory details of the inconsistent and carnal behavior which marked their lives at times.

There are exceptions, such as Abel, Enoch, Samuel, and a few others in whom we would be hard-pressed to find fault. Then there are the others, the majority in fact, whose lifestyles often looked more like a dirty movie than the biographies of Bible characters. Abraham is a prime example. Others are equally questionable by modern church standards.

Noah is listed as a person of great faith, yet the man was found lying in a drunken stupor no sooner than the ground was dry enough for him to fall down on after leaving the ark. In Genesis 8:20, he is seen building an altar shortly after he stepped out of the ark, but in 9:21 he is drunk and naked, apparently involved in some kind of disgusting situation about which Bible scholars have argued for centuries.

Study the lives of the heroes of faith mentioned in Hebrews 11 and take heart. There was Isaac, who committed the same sin as his father, Abraham (see Genesis 26:6-9). Then there is Jacob, who until this day is remembered as a sneaky and conniving man for much of his life. Moses is mentioned, despite the fact that he once killed a man (see Exodus 2:11-12). Samson and David are on the list, even though they both had adulterous affairs which are remembered to this day. Hebrews 11:31 plainly refers to "Rahab the harlot."

If you were to erase the names of those mentioned in Hebrews 11 who had committed shameful sins, it would be a very short chapter. However, God chose not to erase their names when He inspired the writing of Scripture, but instead included them with full knowledge that we would see both their glory days and their gory days. It's almost as if there is a subliminal message contained in that list which says, "Don't think that God doesn't totally love you or that He can't use your life if you have sinned. Look at these people!"

My Sins Were Committed After
I Became a Christian

"You don't understand," Jess said. "I did my crime *after* I became a Christian. It's not like I didn't know what I was doing. I knew it was sin, but at the time I didn't care. I just knew I was tired of feeling poor. As the accountant, I juggled the figures a little to get some extra spending money. Then, when I seemed to get away with it, I increased the amount I was embezzling. I thought my boss was oblivious to what I was doing. Then, for the first time since I had worked there, he decided to have an outside audit done on the company. I had stolen tens of thousands of dollars before I was caught."

Jess hadn't been out of prison very long when I met him. In prison, he had begun to seek the Lord again and now had a great desire for God. As he explained his situation to me, the thing that troubled him was a debilitating sense of guilt about what he had done. He wondered how God could love him, much less use him in any spiritually meaningful way. After all, as he pointed out, he was a Christian when he chose to commit his sin.

You probably haven't been to prison for any of the sins you have committed, but maybe you have had the same kind of nagging accusations in your mind that Jess expressed. In the modern church, we are quick to dismiss sins committed by a person before he became a Christian. Whether the sin was murder, homosexuality, divorce, drugs, adultery, stealing, you name it—it makes no difference. The common response is, "Yes, but that was *before* he became a Christian." The reasoning is absolutely correct. The sins a person committed before he became a believer have been forgiven. They have been permanently and irrevocably removed from us by the cross. God has separated them from us and from Himself as far apart as the east is from the west. It's just like they never happened.

Christians have little problem understanding and accepting that fact...but what about the sins we have committed since then? We aren't so quick to forgive others or ourselves for the sins we have committed since becoming Christians. We have set up a double standard, and it's not difficult to understand why. The reason has to do with our concept of time. It's difficult for us to understand the totality of God's eternal forgiveness for our sins.

Albert Einstein once said, "The distinction between past, present, and future is only an illusion, however persistent." As human beings we live on that illusory time line. Our lifetime is a short segment of a continuum stretching from the creation of all things to the end of time. As time-creatures, we experience events sequentially. However, Einstein was right about time being an illusion. Beyond the time continuum is God, who is not confined by it. He lives in the eternal present and sees all of history from beginning to end. He even sees beyond time, into eternity past in one direction and eternity future in the other. Living beyond time, God views all events as happening simultaneously.[2] Before you were born, God saw the time line of your life. Being omniscient, He knew everything you would ever think, do, or say and yet still chose to save you from your sin and make you His own.

Did God know what Abraham would do in Egypt when He called him to "Go forth from your country...to the land which I will show you" (Genesis 12:1)? Did God know that Noah would get falling-down-drunk as soon as he came off the ark when He told him to build it? Did He know in advance about the sins of Moses, Jacob, Samson, David? Does God know everything about *everybody* in advance? Of course He does, yet He still chooses to call people to Himself.

God knew everything about you before you were even born. Living beyond the constraints of time, He cannot only see everything in your life, He can also deal with it all at once. When you became a Christian, it wasn't just your past sins that were forgiven. *All* the sins of your lifetime were dealt with at the cross (see Colossians 2:13-14), and when Jesus bore them there, they were all still future as they related to time. When you became a believer, your sins were forgiven *in totality*. Every sin you ever *have* or ever *will* commit has been forgiven. It is just as if they never happened!

When a Christian realizes that God's love is so generous that we have already been forgiven for every sin we will ever commit, he begins to discover how His grace "[instructs] us to deny ungodliness and worldly desires and to live sensibly, righteously, and godly" (Titus 2:11). Forgiveness of all our sins is a historical and eternal fact. Not only have we been justified, but we have also already been glorified with Christ in the heavens (see Romans 8:30)! How can it be that we have already been glorified and are seated with Christ? It is because it has been done in the eternal realm. We simply haven't seen it in time yet, but make no mistake about it, it has already been done.

The realization of this fact frees us from condemnation from our past sins and any obligation to future ones. We don't have to walk through life as if we were in a minefield where we may step into temptation and have our faith blown apart. Christians who know their identity in Christ aren't paranoid about sins and temptation. Our responsibility is to simply rest in Christ. How? Christ has called us to simply rest in Him, allowing Him to love us, to live His life through us, and to deal with sins and temptations as they approach us during the short time of our earthly life. He accomplishes His work in us, through the power of His indwelling Spirit who inspires us to respond to His love.

God has forgiven your sins and forgotten them. It's that simple. Don't be hard on yourself—God isn't! The sins you committed after you were born again are in the same category as the ones you committed before you became a Christian—forgiven and forgotten!

How Could God Love Someone Such as Me?

"I do believe that God has forgiven all my sins," Wendy said. "But I'm still struggling about the sins that I don't seem to have victory over yet. I can't accept that He really loves me as much as He would if I turned away from my sins. I'm trying to do better, but I keep failing. I know I must be a disappointment to God." Wendy's perspective is very common among Christians who focus on areas of their lives where they see inconsistency. She believed that God would feel better toward her if she would clean up her act. Is it true that God's feelings toward us are affected by how we behave?

One aspect of the good news of the gospel is that we can bring our weaknesses and sins to God through Christ and openly acknowledge them. We don't have to deny our sins. We don't have to make excuses about them. We don't even need to make promises about how we will try to do better. After all, many of us have learned that we *can't* do better even when we try. When we think we can do better, we are guilty of self-effort rather than faith. Legalism insists that we must improve our behavior for God's sake, but grace gently encourages us to simply own it and then lay it at the foot of the cross. When we see sins in our lifestyle, the best thing we can do with them is to *run* to our heavenly Father and lay them out before Him in all their ugliness with the assurance that "God is to us a God of deliverances" (Psalm 68:20).

I was holding my baby grandson on my lap one day. I was laughing at him to see if I could get him to laugh. It worked. Every time I would laugh, Jonathan saw my delight in him, and he laughed too. As we sat on the couch laughing together, I was filled with emotion and thought to myself, "It's amazing how much love I feel for him."

At that moment a thought came into my mind that I knew was from God: *That's nothing compared to the love that I have for you.* I was overwhelmed by the realization that my heavenly Father loves me infinitely more than I could ever love my grandchildren or children.

As we continued to play together on the couch, I became increasingly aware that Jonathan had "sinned against me." It was a diaper problem—a serious one. Here I was, holding him on my lap, showering him with attention and affection, and he does something like *that!* What do you suppose I did? I didn't throw him from my lap in anger, screaming, "Depart from me, you worker of iniquity!" Not at all. You see, I understand something about babies—they do that kind of thing. I wasn't pleased with his behavior, but what he did changed absolutely nothing between the two of us.

Jonathan will soon outgrow that habit and will begin to act maturely in that area of life. As I later thought about the incident, I was reminded of our Father's patience and lovingkindness toward us. He is always interacting with us with a divine determination to cause us to find pleasure in Him. Yet at the very same time, we sometimes sin against Him. We make a mess of things, despite His continuous commitment to cause all things to work together for our good.

When we sin against Him, does He cast us off? Absolutely not! "For He Himself knows our frame; He is mindful that we are but dust" (Psalm 103:14). When

Jonathan experienced his baby problem—that messy diaper—his mood soon changed from happy to sad. He began to cry, instinctively knowing that he needed some sort of help from somebody bigger than himself. That is what happens in the lives of believers when we sin. We know that Somebody bigger who loves us will take care of our problem and deliver us from whatever it is that we've gotten ourselves into at the moment. We just cry out to Him in dependence and anticipation and He does the rest.

What to Do About Our Sins

If God has forgiven every sin we will ever commit during our lifetime, then how does the Bible tell us to relate to sin? In a word, get over it! It's astounding to see the preoccupation that the modern church has with sin despite the fact that Jesus came "to put away sin by the sacrifice of Himself" (Hebrews 9:26). What Jesus came to *put away*, many modern Christians enjoy discussing, studying, arguing over, rebuking, renouncing, outlining, participating in, and being obsessed with most of the time. If Jesus came to put it away, why do we keep trying to take it back out?

• ***Sometimes we try to take sin back out so that we can experience it.*** Even though believers now possess the righteous nature of Jesus Christ (see Romans 5:17,19), we still must contend with the law of sin, which exists in our bodies (see Romans 7:23). A grace walk *enables* us to experience victory over temptation, but it doesn't eliminate the possibility of sinning.

Is there a sin in your life that you cannot seem to break free from? Legalism offers a thousand answers for things you can *do* to find freedom, but in reality God loves you so much that He has already done everything necessary for you to walk in freedom continuously. The key to freedom is the indwelling life of Jesus Christ. If we are to agree with the finished work of Christ and put away sin, then we must understand that He alone is our victory.

I recently received an e-mail from Stephen, whose mother committed suicide when he was ten years old. Early in life he turned to pornography in an attempt to ease his pain. He describes,

> By the time I was 11 years old, I had become heavily involved in pornography as an attempt to find relief from the pain of my mother's death. But I didn't see it as really that bad. "They're just pictures," I would say to myself.

> When I was in high school, a couple of my buddies explained the gospel to me, and for the first time in my life I saw that I was a sinner, and I needed a Savior. I received Jesus and made a commitment to live for God and obey Him in every area of my life. I sincerely tried to live right, but I was hooked on pornography, and I couldn't will myself to stop. I tried everything. I prayed, fasted, memorized all the Scriptures that have to do with sexual sin, went to deliverance services, paid my tithes (as if I could buy my freedom), witnessed to as many friends as I could, blocked internet porn and 1-900 sex lines. These are just a few of the things I did, but when it was all said and done, I was still in bondage.

> I had decided to commit suicide when a friend of mine suggested I read your book, *Grace Walk*. As God began to teach me who I am in Christ, it began to sink in that the only answer is Christ and the cross. I finally saw it. It is only through the cross that I am free. I was, and am, elated. Thank God, the answer to my problem was not more religious rules (which only lead to condemnation and

death), but instead it is simply God's grace through
Jesus Christ.

Consider what Stephen said happened to him. "As God
began to teach me who I am in Christ, it began to sink in
that the only answer is Christ and the cross." Stephen's
freedom from bondage came as a result of *revelation*.

As he read the truths about Christ's finished work, the
Holy Spirit opened his understanding. A miracle resulted.
Stephen went on to say, "I finally saw it. It is only through
the cross that I am free."

Stephen discovered the reality of God's grace in his
own life. He believed that Christ's life and victory over sin
are what God the Father looks at when He sees Stephen's
life. By faith, Stephen suddenly saw himself for who he is
in Christ. This revelation produced great joy and freedom
from sin.

Is there a besetting sin in your life? Look to Jesus Christ!
He will supply the revelation and the faith that will bring
you the same joy and freedom that Stephen experienced.
God has promised to complete His work in us.

**♦ *Sometimes we try to take sin back out so that we
can experience self-condemnation.*** It is an enigma that
Christians sometimes seem to have an affinity for self-condemnation. An attitude of self-condemnation is nothing
less than an assault on the finished work of Christ by pun-
ishing ourselves for our own sins. To punish ourselves by
self-loathing is to imply that when Jesus declared, "It is finished," He was wrong. "There is still something left for me
to do—detest myself," this attitude of unbelief insists.

Self-condemnation is a sacrament to the Christian
legalist. It's one way he seeks to atone for his sins. His
rationale may be conscious or unconscious, but it suggests
that if he is sorry enough, if he feels bad enough, if he
executes enough emotional self-flagellation and offers up

the sacrifice of genuine self-contempt, *then* God will forgive him.

While his demeanor appears to be one of contrition, in reality his attitude demonstrates the worst kind of pride, which is both gaudy and despicable. He actually thinks that there is something *he* can do to be forgiven. His self-centered attitude of paying his own way with the currency of guilt is an affront to the finished work of Jesus Christ.

He talks a talk that sounds godly to many, but his licentious loathing of himself betrays a brazen and adulterous affair with the law. He may have died to the law so that he could be joined to Jesus Christ (see Romans 7:4), but his insistence on wallowing in the bed of self-judgment with the law suggests a religious hedonism that brings him great pleasure in the darkest places of his flesh.

Jesus came to "put away sin by the sacrifice of *Himself*," says the Bible. If He didn't succeed at that, then our hopes are all in vain. If He did succeed, then any attempt to add our own words of self-condemnation to what the cross has already spoken will only dilute, and thus negate, its power.

Have you sinned against God by allowing yourself to entertain self-condemnation about your sins, past or present? Not only is it unnecessary, but it is a sin itself. Brennan Manning noted, "We would not inflict on our dog the abuse we heap on ourselves."[3] Renounce your sin and run into the loving arms of your heavenly Father, giving up both your sins and your self-condemnation to Him. Lay it all at His feet and allow Him to simply love you. Judgment day for you is finished. It was over at the cross when Jesus declared it to be so. God has nothing to say to you now other than words of love and acceptance. How do you quit your sin? Ask Him to open the eyes and ears of your heart so that you can receive these incredible truths.

I love the way Dr. Charles K. Robinson puts it:

> I know you. I created you. I have loved you from your mother's womb. You have fled—as you now know—from my love, but I love you nevertheless and not-the-less however far you flee. It is I who sustain your very power of fleeing, and I will never finally let you go. I accept you as you are. You are forgiven. I know all your sufferings. I have always known them. Far beyond your understanding, when you suffer, I suffer. I also know all the little tricks by which you try to hide the ugliness you have made of your life from yourself and others. But you are beautiful. You are beautiful more deeply within than you can see. You are beautiful because you yourself, in the unique person that only you are, reflect already something of the beauty of my holiness in a way which shall never end. You are beautiful also because I, and I alone, see the beauty you shall become. Through the transforming power of my love which is made perfect in weakness you shall become perfectly beautiful in a uniquely irreplaceable way, which neither you nor I will work out alone, for we shall work it out together.[4]

My friend, your sin is gone. It is forgiven and forgotten. Past, present, and future sins have all been dealt with by the cross of Jesus Christ. There is now nothing to stand in your way or to prevent you from a continuous, intimate, loving relationship with God. It's true that you *are* beautiful because by your co-crucifixion with Christ, everything that wasn't beautiful was taken away from you.

You are a new creation now (see 2 Corinthians 5:17) and all the old things that could have caused you guilt and anxiety are forever gone. The books have been reconciled on your sins, with an eternal declaration that they have been paid in full. God will never even so much as question you about them. You are free to let them go now.

Don't waste your energy on something which God has forgotten. Instead, simply enjoy Him, completely free from every trace of guilt and condemnation.

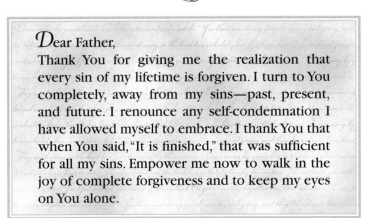

*D*ear Father,
Thank You for giving me the realization that every sin of my lifetime is forgiven. I turn to You completely, away from my sins—past, present, and future. I renounce any self-condemnation I have allowed myself to embrace. I thank You that when You said, "It is finished," that was sufficient for all my sins. Empower me now to walk in the joy of complete forgiveness and to keep my eyes on You alone.

G.R.A.C.E. GROUP QUESTIONS

1. Read the story of Abraham and Sarah's trip to Egypt in Genesis 12:10-20. What are the implications about God's grace in their story? Think of modern-day examples of people who have committed great sins and yet have gone on to be used by God. In what ways can you relate their story to your own life?

2. Read the list of names given in Hebrews 11 as heroes of faith. Identify the specific sins committed by each one, as recorded in the Bible. How did they overcome those sins?

3. Discuss how the issue of total forgiveness for the sins of our lifetime can best be taught in church. Read and explain Colossians 2:13-14 in your own words. What other Bible verses substantiate that Christians are completely forgiven?

4. What was suggested in this chapter concerning what a Christian can do when he is aware of sin in his own life? What would you say to a person who is guilt-ridden about sins committed *after* he became a Christian?

5. Why is self-condemnation an insult to the finished work of Jesus Christ on the cross? What Bible verses would you show a person who is struggling with self-condemnation?

6. Read Hebrews 9:26 and discuss what it means that Jesus came "to put away sin." In what sense has He put it away?

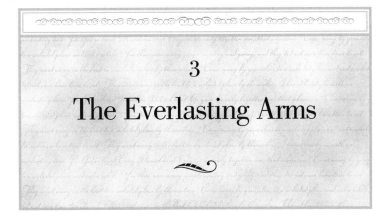

3
The Everlasting Arms

A FAMOUS PRESIDENT OF A FUNDAMENTALIST Bible college once said that if he had his whole life to do over again, he wouldn't change one thing he had ever done. I find his statement to be puzzling. I wonder how any man could say that and mean it! Was every decision he made the perfect one? I can't speak for his track record, but I know that I've done some dumb things in my life, things I definitely would do differently if I had them to do over again.

There was the time shortly after I was married that I decided I was being called to New York City to work with an organization that ministered to street people. I convinced my young bride, Melanie, that this was our divine calling, and then, as an "act of faith," proceeded to sell every single item we owned except our bed and refrigerator (the two most important home furnishings for a newlywed). A few months later, when the New York ministry declined my offer to come and help, we found ourselves living in an almost empty house for quite some time.

That's only one of my many blunders in life. I won't list them all, lest you think I'm a complete idiot. I share this one from my early adult life to illustrate the point that sincere Christians can sometimes make foolish decisions. Unlike my desire to move to New York, some of our impulsive decisions actually materialize. We act on them, then later wonder if we can ever be all that we could have been had we not made those foolish choices.

Ruth approached me after I spoke at her church one day and said, "I have never felt the kind of closeness to God that I want. I believe the reason is my marriage. I married my husband at an early age. I had hardly even dated anybody else. Our relationship has been rocky for the entire 20 years we've been married. I had planned to be a missionary before I met him. I've sometimes wondered if my decision to marry was an impulsive mistake made by a young girl who really was experiencing nothing more than being in love with love. I have always felt that God was disappointed with me for not becoming a missionary."

The Effect of Mistakes in Life

Ruth believed that she had made a choice which would prevent her from experiencing God's best for her as long as she lived. It's not that she chose to sin against God. She believed it was an honest mistake, but thought that her one wrong choice would somehow negatively affect the rest of her life and that she would always have to settle for God's second best, wondering what might have been.

This attitude is a subtle trick the enemy uses to keep the Christian from experiencing deep intimacy with God. After all, how can we have a close, loving, and transparent relationship with someone who can't forget a mistake we made, someone who reminds us that what we did can never be undone and that our action required him to change *his* plans?

Intimacy with God is challenging if you believe that you've made an irrevocable mistake that has brought His disapproval. When we've made choices that we believe have fouled things up, it's hard to have confidence that God will still give us His very best. We tend to think that even though He will bless us, it won't be as good as it might have been. We blame ourselves, and thus, focus on our *self*. This kind of attitude will negatively interfere with how we perceive God's love for us and His plan for our life.

Have you made decisions that you believe might have messed up the way your life *could* have been? If so, there is good news that can set you free from that damaging perspective. The news is that *God's love is bigger than your mistakes!* No mistake you have ever made or ever could make will cause your life to jump track.

You belong to God, and it is His responsibility, not yours, to ensure that you stay the course. That fact is inherent to the very meaning of the word *grace*, which suggests it's all up to Him, not you. You may make apparent detours in life, but God's love for you is so great that He won't allow you to veer off His assigned path and wander out of His will for your life.

A Sovereign God

The Psalmist said that "The Lord has established His throne in the heavens, And His sovereignty rules over all" (Psalm 103:19). This world doesn't exist in a cosmic setting in which events happen by chance. Everything in existence functions under the superintending guidance of a sovereign God. On the grand scale, "By Him all things were created, both in the heavens and on earth, visible and invisible, whether thrones or dominions or rulers or authorities—all things have been created through Him and for Him" (Colossians 1:16).

God is a big God who has everything under control. The stars don't hang in the sky on nothingness. They are held there by the omnipotent will of a sovereign God. The tide on the beach doesn't coincidentally stop at its boundaries and return to the sea. It is ordered back by divine design. The earth doesn't keep spinning on its axis under its own momentum. God designed it that way.

However, this same God who attends to the majestic details of the universe also gives meticulous attention to the minutiae of life. For instance, the Bible says that He has the hairs of your head numbered. That's serious attention to detail! Not one baby bird falls out of its nest apart from His attention (see Matthew 10:29-30). He is God of both the macroscopic and the microscopic. Nothing is too big or too small to be beyond His direct control.

When we consider that man is God's crowning touch in creation and that Christians in particular are His divine workmanship (see Ephesians 2:10), we can be assured that God is "up close and personal" in the affairs of your life. The Bible says that God "ponders" all your goings (see Proverbs 5:21 NKJV). The word denotes the idea of somebody walking alongside you with His face inches away from yours, carefully examining, scrutinizing, analyzing every move you make. Not only does God ponder your actions, but He even ponders your attitudes and the motivations that cause you to do the things you do (see Proverbs 21:2). Make no mistake about it, God has His eye on you and always has and always will.

There is not one person who is *continuously* on my mind, but you are never out of God's conscious thought or away from His immediate attention. He has been obsessed with you for all eternity and can't take His mind off you. He is so in love with you that He has committed all the resources at His disposal (which are considerable) to your well-being. God has never glanced away from you for a moment.

The author of lies, the great Deceiver, Satan himself, would like you to believe that you have made choices which now negatively affect how God relates to you or limit the extent to which He can use your life for His glory. However, the Word of God teaches us just the opposite. The prophet Daniel saw it clearly when he said that all the inhabitants of the earth add up to nothing when compared to God's divine determination. He wrote that God "does according to His will in the host of heaven and among the inhabitants of earth; And no one can ward off His hand" (Daniel 4:35).

I remember a time before I understood this truth when I was scolding myself for a wrong choice I had made. I thought, *Because of my own foolishness, God can't do the thing He* obviously *had planned!* At that moment, another thought popped into my head that answered, *Don't kid yourself. You're not that strong.* I think I know whose voice that was, don't you? God will do what God wants to do, and we flatter ourselves when we think we are big enough to stop it.

If God isn't in charge of *everything*, then how can we know He is in charge of *anything*? Timothy said that He is the "Only Sovereign, the King of kings and Lord of lords" (1 Timothy 6:15). That's a clear explanation of the fact that He is the One in charge. He asks nobody's permission or advice for anything. He does what He wants and doesn't have to explain His reasoning to us.

There is much about God's sovereignty I don't understand—why He allows some things and prevents others. With no disrespect or irreverence intended, I'll admit that if I were in charge, I would often do things differently. But I'm not in charge—He is. We will never fully understand His unseen motives and methods.

If we were able to completely understand God and His ways, our minds could contain Him, and God can't be contained. Contemporary religion generally presents a God who is forced to submit to modern rationale, values, and predictable patterns of behavior. It markets a manageable God, offering the commodity of a comfortable, devotional experience—warm fuzzies on demand. On the other hand, the God of the Bible isn't like that. Our God is beyond our control, sometimes displaying wild passion for those He loves and at other times appearing to have gone on a permanent vacation when we need Him most. Regardless of how hard we may try, we simply can't figure Him out.

God exists in what an anonymous author from the fourteenth century called "The Cloud of Unknowing." His frame of reference is so beyond ours that we simply can't consistently understand His ways in this world or even in our own life. Even the most spiritually mature among us often find themselves asking, "What's God up to here? What is going on in this situation? What does this circumstance mean?"

Sometimes we can look backward in time, see what He was doing, and understand His ways, even though they didn't make sense at the time. However, many of life's mysteries are beyond our understanding. God's grace equips us to trust in His sovereign control. Our faith then frees us from wallowing in constant frustration, confusion, and self-doubt. We can walk in His faithfulness and trust His ways even when they aren't our ways.

The Arms of God

We begin to trust God and His sovereignty as we understand the depth of His love for those who are in Christ. Because you are in Him, He has all the bases of your life covered regardless of what decisions you have already made or are yet to make. If the fundamental message of Scripture were to be reduced to two simple words, they would be "in Christ," a phrase used 77 times in the New Testament.

Contemporary teaching on Christianity often focuses on *Christ* being in *our* lives, but the emphasis of the New Testament is that *we* have entered into *His* life. "In Him we live and move and exist," wrote Luke (see Acts 17:28). By the cross, God has put to death the old life we had (see Galatians 2:20; Romans 6:1-7; Colossians 3:3) and has now given us the very life of Jesus Christ to be our own.

God loves you so much that He has brought you to Himself, where you will stay in Christ for all eternity. Your choices do not keep you there. It's His decision. Through His grace, we have come home to rest in Him. When Moses announced God's blessing on the tribes of Israel by promising to bring them into His place of rest, He told them that "the eternal God is a dwelling place, and underneath are the everlasting arms" (Deuteronomy 33:27).

Christians are in Christ, says the Bible, *and underneath are the everlasting arms.* Do you know what it means to have God's everlasting arms underneath you? Whenever I read this verse, I associate it with a memory from my childhood.

I was at a Sunday school class party, and everybody there except me seemed to know how to swim. My teacher, noticing that I was in the shallow end of the pool, asked, "Steve, can't you swim?"

"No," I answered, embarrassed.

"Do you want me to teach you?" he asked. I agreed, and he began his instruction. "The first thing you need to know," he said, "is that you don't have to be afraid of sinking and drowning. If you relax, your body *will* float. Just try lying on your back and relaxing in the water." I lay back in the water, attempting to do what he had told me.

However, every time I lay back and felt the water filling my ears, I would lift my head. Then I would begin to sink. "Don't lift your head," my teacher encouraged me. "Just relax and let your ears go underwater. You won't sink." Again I would try to take his advice, but when I felt the water rising above my ears toward my face, I would rise up and again begin to sink.

Finally he said, "Lie back *in my arms* and I will hold you on top of the water so that you won't sink." I began to lie back, and true to his word, I felt his arms underneath me, holding me up. As he held me there and I felt the support of his arms, I began to relax a little. After a short time, I was comfortable. Finally, he said to me, "Okay, now I'm going to move my arms from your back so that you won't feel me touching you, but *they will still be beneath you,* and I will catch you if you start to sink. Do you trust me?" he asked. I expressed that I did trust him, and he did exactly what he said. For the first time in my life, I floated on the water. I felt no fear because I knew that underneath me were his arms. I knew that I had his guarantee that he would not let me sink.

There have been times in my life when decisions I made caused me to say to myself, "Oh no, I'm sunk now!" My assessment always proved to be wrong. Whether I felt them or not, underneath me were God's everlasting arms, keeping me from sinking. The same is true of your life. You are where you are today because God has upheld you by His arms. The arms of God provide a lifetime guarantee that He will take care of the details of our lives, ensuring that we won't make choices that cause us to sink to a place He doesn't want us to be. You can relax and enjoy the water because God has you in His arms.

What kind of arms does God have? The Bible speaks often about His arms and gives us some insight into the

Person in Whom we are placing our trust. Consider these biblical descriptions of the arms of God:

♦ ***God has outstretched arms.*** This is the most common description of God's arms used in Scripture. To say that the arms of God are outstretched is to suggest that God is not passive about the affairs of our lives, but is actively involved, orchestrating events for our good and His glory. The majority of times that the arms of God are described in Scripture as being stretched out refer to His works on behalf of those whom He loves, rescuing them from circumstances that could potentially destroy them.

One day, when we get to heaven, we will finally recognize the many times God reached out His arms to rescue us from disaster. The Psalmist often wrote songs honoring God for the many times He had delivered him from danger. Have you ever paused to identify the times when God did the same for you? Sit down alone with a note pad sometime, and ask the Lord to show you the many times He has rescued you from disaster. You may be surprised by the swelling sense of joy and gratitude you feel as God reveals how often He has acted on your behalf. This simple exercise may cause you to *feel* a much greater sense of God's loving concern for you.

♦ ***God has strong arms.*** Reflecting upon the frequent times God had delivered Israel, David wrote, "You have a strong arm [and] your hand is mighty!" (Psalm 89:13-14). Well-meaning people sometimes die trying to save others who are drowning. It isn't that their intention isn't good. They simply lack the strength to intervene and pull the person in distress from the water. Consequently, they both drown. Our God always knows when we have gotten in over our heads, He has the loving desire to rescue us, and He has the strength to get the job done!

Have your choices brought you to the place where you don't think you're going to survive your circumstances? Take courage by knowing that the One who loves you has the muscle to deliver you and He has prepared these circumstances for your highest good! When the Apostle Peter found himself in water over his head, the Bible says that, "beginning to sink, he cried out, 'Lord, save me!' *Immediately* Jesus stretched out His hand and took hold of him" (Matthew 14:30-31, emphasis added). The Lord was teaching Peter the lesson of faith and showing him the hopelessness of depending on self.

The One who ponders your every move is always at work on your behalf. What if you failed to ask? He could never stand by and watch you drown in a sea of wrong decisions, despite the fact that at times you may feel otherwise. You can trust that God's strong arm is always reaching out on your behalf.

♦ *God has bare arms.* Isaiah said that "The LORD has comforted His people, He has...bared His holy arm" (Isaiah 52:9-10). God's involvement in your life is not casual. His arm is bare because He has rolled up His sleeves to go to work in your circumstances. Through the eyes of faith, see this all-powerful God—the One who spoke the world into existence, the One who with a word will destroy Satan, the One by Whom all things in this world exist—see *that* God working hard on your behalf!

Don't think for a minute that foolish choices you may have made can overrule the plans divinely devised by this strong bare-armed God who reaches out His strong arm into your circumstances to work out His purposes. While it is true that there is an enemy who would ruin the perfect plan God has for our lives, God *will not allow it*. As Martin Luther wrote in 1529,

And though this world, with devils filled,
    should threaten to undo us,
We will not fear, for God hath willed
    His truth to triumph through us:
The Prince of Darkness grim, we tremble not for him;
His rage we can endure, for lo, his doom is sure,
One little word shall fell him.

If you want to *experience* the depths of intimacy with God through Jesus Christ, it is important to know and believe the truth concerning God's sovereign strength over your life. Although you may still have questions that begin with, "Yes, but what about…?", I encourage you not to try to figure out all the answers before you affirm your total trust in God. Either He is in charge or He is not. Which do you believe? Perhaps it will be necessary for you to pause and pray, repenting of the sin of unbelief. Maybe it will be necessary to acknowledge that you have believed the lie that your choices are capable of thwarting God's eternal purposes for your life.

Many Christians continue to experience spiritual bondage by believing the lie that they have made wrong choices which cannot be overcome. Before I understood the truth of our loving Father's sovereignty, I would sometimes say, "You can't unscramble eggs." But the truth of the matter is that God *can* unscramble eggs! He takes the choices you've made and orchestrates them into the symphony of life that He has written for you. I indicated at the beginning of this chapter that there are things I would do differently if I had them to do over again. It's true, *I* would. However, I can't write the story over again. Given that fact, I must choose to simply rest with confidence in the One who directs this unfolding McVey drama. I don't understand some things about my own story, but one day I will. Until then, my only viable option is to *trust*.

Someone has noted that even the most beautiful tapestries have dark threads interwoven within the pattern made by the designer. God takes the dark threads of foolish choices you have made and uses them in the tapestry of your life. He is not limited by anything you have ever done. Nothing catches Him by surprise. The Bible says that in God's book there were "written all the days that were ordained for [you], when as yet there was not one of them" (Psalm 139:16). Someone once asked, "Did it ever occur to you that nothing ever occurs to God?" We simply aren't big enough to spoil the story of our lives that God has written.

When Christians get to heaven and enjoy by sight the reality of the union we now share with Christ by faith, we will clearly see that our lives are nothing less than a love story depicting the intimate relationship we have with Jesus. As with any love story, there are highs and lows while the story unfolds. There are times when one following the saga might wonder if the lovers' relationship is going to last. Will he be able to keep her? Will she turn away and give her love to another? However, the author of the story knows full well how it is all going to end because he decreed it to be so. Those who watch may be alarmed at times during the telling of the tale, but not the author. He simply enjoys the expression of his own creative skills as the drama is played out before him. He knows that in reality, the story is already finished.

While we move through the divine drama of our lifetime on earth, there will be peaks and valleys. There will be times when we think we have made choices which spoil the whole story, but the Author and Finisher of our faith has already completed His work and has sat down to enjoy the fruit of His labor. (See Hebrews 12:2.) As participants in the divine romance, we will enjoy this time-bound segment of the story much more if we simply believe that He indeed has finished writing the script and will see to it we are on our mark and know our lines *by heart.*

---

*D*ear Father,

I recognize that You are indeed sovereign over my life. I acknowledge that decisions I have made in my lifetime aren't more powerful than Your love for me. I give myself completely to You—my past choices, my present circumstances, my future life. I simply want to live out the love story You have written for You and me. From now on, I won't flatter myself by thinking that I'm the one writing this story. I will simply look to You for direction from day to day and then trust Your loving guidance in my life. You are totally in charge. Thank You for causing me to understand that fact.

G.R.A.C.E. GROUP QUESTIONS

1. Discuss a major decision that you would choose differently if you had it to do over again. List two positive results of that decision that God worked into your circumstances. Discuss the concept of God's love being bigger than our wrong choices.

2. Read Psalm 103:19 and Daniel 4:35 and paraphrase what they say. How can these verses be reconciled with all the wrong present in the world today?

3. Read Deuteronomy 33:27. Describe a time in your life when you were acutely aware of God's everlasting arms beneath you.

4. This chapter points to verses which describe God's arms as being outstretched, strong, and bare. What other verses in the Bible mention God's arms, and what do those verses teach us about Him?

5. Describe the highs and lows of your own personal drama (your life), and explain how you can see God's presence in each of those moments.

4

The Heavenly Hug

SEPTEMBER 11, 2001 WILL FOREVER BE REMEMBERED as the darkest day in our nation's history to date. In an instant, thousands of lives were snuffed out by cowardly actions orchestrated by one man on the other side of the world. When President Bush called our nation to prayer, one lady responded to a CNN news interviewer saying, "Pray? To whom? To a God who would stand by and watch something like this happen without stopping it? I will *not* pray!"

As things progressed in the immediate days that followed the terrorists' attacks, there were more public prayers said and more said about prayer than anytime in recent American history. While this cynic's attitude wasn't representative of most of the people in our country, it did reflect a pervasive and nagging question in many people's minds, including Christians'. It is the age-old question that asks how a loving God could allow such horror to happen to so many innocent people.

Why does a sovereign God appear to sit idly by and watch while tragic events happen in this world? In a message at the National Cathedral in Washington, D.C., three days after the attack on our country, on a day our President designated as a "Day of Prayer and Remembrance," Dr. Billy Graham said:

> How do we understand something like this? Why does God allow evil like this to take place? Perhaps that is what you are asking right now. You may even be angry at God. I want to assure you that God understands these feelings that you may have. We've seen so much on our television, heard on our radio—stories that bring tears to our eyes and make us all feel a sense of anger. But God can be trusted, even when life seems at its darkest.

"God can be trusted, even when life seems at its darkest." Do you believe that to be true? Can we honestly believe that God loves us when life itself seems to be imploding? Perhaps there is no time in our lives that we *feel* less loved by God than when we are facing days of overwhelming difficulties. It doesn't take tragedy on a national scale for the average Christian to wonder about the legitimacy of God's compassion.

Facing a particularly hard personal problem in his life, a friend said to me one day, "I wouldn't let *my* children go through something like this if I had the power to prevent it. So why is God allowing me to face this problem if He loves me and has the power to stop it?" The question is a legitimate one and deserves an answer. How can we experience genuine intimacy with a God Who allows us to go through personal circumstances that sometimes threaten to shake the very foundation of our faith? When a person is hurting and his faith seems to offer no relief from the pain, what is he to conclude about God's love?

Jesus once said, "You will know the truth, and the truth will make you free" (John 8:32). What is the truth about how God's love for us is related to the personal pain we will experience in our lives? There are several strands in the cord of divine truth concerning suffering which offer a lifeline of hope for ongoing intimacy with God in the midst of life's unavoidable adversities.

Welcome to Planet Earth

The seed of sin planted in this world in the garden of Eden continues to bear fruit to the present day. In the general sense, human suffering is a result of the fall of man. When we get home to heaven there won't be any more pain (see Revelation 21:4), but for the time being we still live on foreign soil where pain goes with the territory. Living as a foreigner is not easy; we must learn how to adapt. For example, my wife, Melanie, has always detested seafood, but when we visit Asian countries, where fish is a staple of their diet, she simply has to deal with it. There is no other choice. When you are in the culture, you adapt.

Pain is a part of the cultural fiber of this short earth-life, and no amount of faith is going to make it go away. Standing at ground zero in his own personal disaster, Job once noted that "man is born for trouble, as sparks fly upward" (Job 5:7). He recognized that, at best, life "is short-lived and full of turmoil" (Job 14:1).

The fact that one may be a Christian doesn't exempt him from problems. Jesus Himself said, "In the world, you have tribulation, but take courage; I have overcome the world" (John 16:33). Faith in Christ doesn't insulate us from the stinging experiences of life. It does, however, equip us to face our problems with confidence that His loving attention will guide us through those difficult circumstances. Faith seldom answers the "why" of our problems, but instead offers the answer to "how" we can survive our circumstances.

"Steve, you need to get to the hospital immediately. There's been an accident." The words caused my blood to run cold. "Andrew has fallen at work...broken back... brain hemorrhage..." My wife's words trailed off beyond my conscious thoughts as my mind struggled to comprehend what I was hearing about my son. I hung up the telephone and rushed from my office to the hospital.

"The situation is very serious," the doctor told us. "Our hospital isn't prepared to handle extensive injuries of this nature, so we are transferring him to a hospital that is better equipped." In the moments that followed, we learned that our 20-year-old son had fallen through an open stairwell on the construction site where he was working. We were told that it might be days before the long-term effects of his injury would be known. He could be paralyzed; he might be mentally incapacitated; he may not even live. These were the possibilities outlined to us in a short conference with the doctor before we got into our car to follow the ambulance that carried him.

As we drove across town in silence, tears streamed down our cheeks. I had commented at times over the years about how suddenly life can change, but this was one scenario I had never imagined. As we pulled into the emergency room parking lot and stopped the car, I reached over and took Melanie's hand. She looked up at me through teary eyes.

"We don't know what's going to happen in here today," I said. "Andrew may not live. He may be a paraplegic. He might be mentally retarded from now on. But before we go in here, can agree on one thing? No matter what happens with all of this—can we go into this hospital agreeing that God is God, and God is good?" Melanie nodded her head, indicating yes. We got out of the car and walked into the hospital, holding hands.

The days that followed were not easy ones. Andrew bled inside his swelling brain for several days. There was a 12-hour operation on his broken back. There were 30 days in the hospital, followed by three long years of therapy. To the glory of God, He did recover and today lives a normal lifestyle with little residual effects from the accident.

"Why *me?*" we may sometimes be tempted to ask, but the more logical question is, "Why *not* me?" "Accidents" happen, people are injured, and sometimes they even die. Being a Christian won't prevent these kinds of circumstances. To believe that trusting Christ will shield us from suffering is to misunderstand how life works. It is an erroneous belief which will cause doubt and confusion when troubles do come—as they most certainly will.

God's Final Answer

In the midst of painful circumstances, we can still know intimacy with God by recognizing an important fact—our circumstances are *not* an indication of how God feels about us. If we believe that our present situation in life is indicative of God's love for us, we will become disheartened and wonder if God is absent when troubles come. Paul spoke to the issue of how our troubles relate to God's love for us in Romans 8:38-39:

> For I am convinced that neither death, nor life, nor angels, nor principalities, nor things present, nor things to come, nor powers, nor height, nor depth, nor any other created thing, will be able to separate us from the love of God, which is in Christ Jesus our Lord.

God's final word on how He feels about you is revealed by the finished work of Jesus Christ on the cross, not by whatever circumstances you may face. Jesus Himself was "a man of sorrows, and acquainted with grief" (Isaiah 53:3). If you want to understand God's attitude toward you, stare into the face of the Crucified One, Who proved that He would rather die than live without you. By choice, He committed Himself to the cruelty of crucifixion, driven there by a divine passion for you that set His heart ablaze with resolve to do whatever was necessary to ensure that you would be His forever. The strongest strand in the cord of truth that will sustain any Christian who suffers is the realization that Jesus Christ loves you with an eternal passion that can never be extinguished or even diminished.

Experiencing Him in Our Suffering

Salvation is not a matter of Jesus Christ coming into *our* lives. That perspective is egocentric because it makes man the focal point in regeneration. To become a Christian means that we enter into *His* life. Our old life is put to death (see Galatians 2:20; Romans 6:1-6; Colossians 3:3), and we then receive the indwelling Christ, in Whom we live from that day forward (see Acts 17:28).

Few Christians resist the biblical teaching that Christ wants to express His life through them. We believe in living victoriously, possessing spiritual peace, and experiencing supernatural power. All of these are indeed characteristic of the lifestyle of those who abide in Christ, but there is another trait of His life that lacks luster to many modern Christians. It is the element of suffering.

When you entered into Christ, you came into union with every aspect of His life. Suffering is not an insignificant part of living in Him; it is one of the most effective ways that the Holy Spirit teaches us our true identity in Christ. It is often through suffering that God carries us deeper and deeper into an understanding of who we are in Him and Who He is in us. How does this occur? Perhaps an illustration from my own life will help explain.

Several years ago I had taken an early-morning shower. I slid the shower door open to step out, when somehow it suddenly jumped off its track. The door instantly fell with its edge landing straight across the top of my big toe like a guillotine (I probably wouldn't become a war hero in battle if this experience is indicative of my potential).

When the door hit my toe, I felt a mental jolt in my brain as if someone had just shot me in the head. I looked down at my toe and saw a deep gash, which was now pouring out blood. I jumped out of the shower and into the bedroom on one foot, and knowing I was going to need stitches, called for Melanie.

I'm glad my wife already adored me, because when she walked into the bedroom and saw a naked, soaking-wet man with an anguished expression, jumping up and down on one foot while holding the other with both hands, blood gushing from between his fingers...it probably didn't do anything to validate my masculinity to her. With Melanie's help, I dried off, put on my clothes, and drove to the hospital emergency room, where the doctor stitched my toe.

When that shower door cut my toe, everything else in life lost its significance to me. I didn't care about conflicts in the Middle East, famine in Africa, or even the spiritual condition of our own country. Only one thing mattered to me at that moment. You might say that right then, my whole life was a big toe. My all-consuming thought was, "I need a doctor *now*." I didn't want to bleed to death and have to tell the martyrs in heaven that I got there because of a toe cut by a shower door. I've never read about anybody being laughed out of heaven, and I didn't want to be the first.

Seriously, though the incident seems humorous now, it wasn't funny at the time. My pain served one purpose with extreme efficiency—it caused me to want to see the doctor. That's the way real suffering works in the lives of Christians. Suffering causes the believer to become consumed with the desire to experience Jesus Christ! It makes us want to see Him, to hear His voice, to feel His touch in our circumstances. This strand in the cord of eternal truth about suffering will sustain the Christian who clings to it. Our pain points us toward Jesus Christ!

Suffering brings the indwelling life of Christ into our lives in a *manifest* way, enabling us to sense Him, to *see* Him by faith in ways that are seldom experienced in calmer days. When I cut my toe, I became oblivious to everything except my immediate need and my desire for the one who could meet that need.

So it is in our grace walk. God uses the severe problems of life to focus our attention on Jesus. The believer's thoughts turn to Christ in times of suffering as naturally as my thoughts turned toward the doctor when I had my accident. Suffering has a way of immediately distancing us from the superfluous, incidental matters of life that distract us from Jesus Christ. When a believer hurts, deep from within, at the very core of his being, is the heartfelt cry, *"Abba!* Daddy!" (see Romans 8:15).

When *Abba's* babies hurt, He is intensively involved. Sometimes our pain is so great that it cannot be clearly expressed in words. At other times, we just don't have the energy to speak. People who aren't feeling well often want assistance, but when a person is *critically* ill, they sometimes want to be left alone despite the fact that they may need intensive care. When we cry out to *Abba*, He hears, but there are other times when we can't even cry out for His help. At those times,

> the Spirit also helps our weakness; for we do not know how to pray as we should, but the Spirit Himself intercedes for us with groanings too deep for words; and He [*Abba*] who searches the hearts knows what the mind of the Spirit is, because He intercedes for the saints according to the will of God. And we know that God causes all things to

work together for good to those who love God, to those who are called according to His purpose (Romans 8:26-28).

God loves you so much that He will *always* work in your circumstances when you suffer. Don't think that because He doesn't eliminate the problem, help isn't being given. Sometimes His most helpful acts in our lives occur when He goes *through* our circumstances with us instead of delivering us out of them. I have sometimes prayed, "Father, this hurts too much for it to be wasted. Please accomplish the maximum good in this situation that can be done."

The Revelation of His Glory

God's goal when we suffer is that Christ's life within us may be manifested. As Watchman Nee pointed out, it is only when the alabaster box containing the precious, aromatic ointment is *broken* that its beautiful fragrance can fill the environment (see Mark 14:3-9). God continually works to break us of any hope that *we* have life under control so that we will experience life under *His* control. It's in this breaking process, facilitated by suffering, that self-reliance is set aside and the fragrance of Christ is released from within.

If you have ever prayed for God to use your life for His glory, you shouldn't be surprised when suffering comes. As in the days of John the Baptist, "He must increase and [we] must decrease." That decrease only happens as we hand over to God the deed to our lives, surrendering complete ownership, including all our trials and suffering, to Him. God loves us so much that He will rescue us from *ourselves*. It's often a cruel irony that the enemy whispers to us during our trials, telling us that God must not care when, in reality, the reason for our pain is that God *does* care.

The Apostle Peter wrote:

> Beloved, do not be surprised at the fiery ordeal among you, which comes upon you for your testing, as though some strange thing were happening to you; but to the degree that you share the sufferings of Christ, keep on rejoicing; so that also at the revelation of His glory you may rejoice with exaltation (1 Peter 4:12-13).

It's normal for the believer who hungers for God to experience suffering, for in his pain he will come to know "the revelation of His glory." What is this glory that Peter said will cause us to become so excited that we can't contain ourselves once it is revealed to us? The Apostle Paul defined this glory when he wrote, "*Christ in you*, the hope of glory" (Colossians 1:27, emphasis added). This revelation happens when the Holy Spirit causes the Christian to supernaturally understand the reality of his union with Jesus. Christ is not simply *in* your life; He *is* your life!

When we understand that Christ is our life, we can face anything. We come to realize that we can do all things through Christ, Who strengthens us. Our fiery trials become the backdrop upon which the life of Jesus Christ can be seen in us in the same way that a brilliant diamond best reflects its beauty against a black background.

Sometimes suffering is renounced and rebuked under the guise of faith, but this approach is a contradiction of Christian orthodoxy. The Apostle Paul prayed to "know Him and the power of His resurrection *and the fellowship of His suffering*" (Philippians 3:10, emphasis added). What Paul prayed *for*, many today pray *against*. Why did Paul pray to know His suffering? It's because He knew that suffering is a greenhouse in which *fellowship* with Jesus Christ can flourish.

Heavenly Hugs

Suffering creates an environment which often proves to be extremely conducive for intimacy with God. There's something about serious trouble that sensitizes us to God's presence. Problems reduce life to its most basic elements. Our troubles often take us by the hand and lead us to the foot of the cross. In that sense, suffering may become our best friend at times. Never are we more fully participating in the life of Jesus Christ than when we share in His sufferings.

When you hurt, Jesus Christ grieves with you in your pain. Don't make the mistake of believing that if God really cared, He would deliver you out of your painful situation. Remember that He didn't even rescue *Jesus* from the cross as He suffered, because He knew its ultimate purpose—our salvation. God loves you so much that He won't take away the pain if it serves a greater purpose in your life. Instead, He will walk the path of pain with you, and in the person of the Comforter (see John 14:16 KJV) will sustain you each step of the way.

One effective tool the enemy uses against the believer is the lie that God must not care about our problems. However, when we are in the midst of suffering, it's important to affirm the truth declared by the Psalmist, "This I know, that God is for me" (Psalm 56:9). Reflect on that truth for a moment—God is *for me*. Do you really believe that? Once we have embraced the truth that God is for us, the details of our circumstances become subordinate to the realization that God both cares about and controls our lives.

That foundational understanding of God's concern for us then becomes the platform upon which intimacy with Him can rest. When we honestly believe that God knows and *cares* about every detail of our lives, when we understand that He is deeply touched by our weaknesses (see Hebrews 4:15), when we are convinced that He hurts when we hurt, when we *know* these things, intimate fellowship with Him will be the natural experience in our pain. Jesus Christ longs for you to *feel* His love at the darkest times of your life.

A few years ago a dear friend of mine experienced a horror that would be every husband's worst nightmare. Fred awakened one morning to discover that his young wife, Rachel, lay dead in the bed beside him. She hadn't been sick and had no known health problems. She simply went to bed one night and never woke up.

I shed tears when I heard the news of Rachel's death and then immediately began to pray for Fred. I couldn't help but project myself into his circumstance and wonder how I would survive if such a horrible thing happened to me. To awaken and find that your mate has died beside you during the night is beyond comprehension for most of us.

Having lunch with Fred one day, I asked him how he was doing. I was moved by the story he told me about Jesus comforting him during one of his darkest days. "From the beginning, part of me has wanted to be alone, and yet at the same time, I have craved people and attention," Fred said. "I have felt lonely even in a crowd. Like Job, I asked God why, but He was silent in my despair. I have felt His presence in the love of my family and friends."

He continued, "About a week after Rachel's death, I had dinner in the home of close friends. They showered me with love and attention, and their young children lavished their affection on me. I left for home that evening encouraged and praising God for giving me so many close friends. But when I went to bed that night, my emotions changed. I couldn't sleep. It was a very cold December, and I was shivering and praying, struggling with deep despair. All I could do was to cry out from my broken heart, 'God, I need your help!'"

Fred's eyes brimmed with tears as he continued his story. "Suddenly, at that moment, I *felt* God's presence beside me. I was lying on my side and I knew He was right beside me. His arms *embraced* me, and a warm ocean current flowed throughout my whole body. The sensation was brief, but I felt a closeness to Him that I can't describe. I was at peace for the first time in over a week, and I was able to drift off to a restful sleep. I awoke the next morning, praising God for revealing Himself to me. From that moment, I somehow knew that I could trust Him in all of my sorrow. I realized that God hadn't chosen to save me *from* my adversity, but would ultimately lead me out of it. I realize now that God was working and answering my prayer, when I could see nothing but darkness."

In the arms of Jesus, Fred found the peace He so desperately needed after his wife's death. Have you ever experienced the hug of Jesus? He *wants* you to feel His love in every circumstance of life. I have heard some spiritual leaders caution believers about the danger of an overemphasis on feelings in our walk with God. While this may be a legitimate danger at times, I am convinced that many have gone to the opposite extreme and *excluded* feelings from our relationship with Christ.

The presence of the Christ who indwells us impacts us at every level of our being. To cognitively know that we are loved by somebody else is one thing. To *feel* that love is another matter altogether. Healthy, loving relationships impact our thoughts *and* emotions. At times when we feel like life has run over us, we need more than a rational answer. We need a hug. Jesus always stands ready to give us the emotional comfort we want.

On the day that Billy Graham spoke to our nation after the attack on the World Trade Center and the Pentagon, he closed his remarks with these words: "My prayer today is that we will feel the loving arms of God wrapped around us and will know in our hearts that He will never forsake us as we trust in Him." His prayer acknowledged the need we all have when tragedy comes—a loving embrace from our heavenly Father.

When standing in the middle of troubling and confusing circumstances, choose to reflect on the reality of the love of Christ for you. Through the eyes of faith, envision Jesus wrapping His arms around you. He hugs you and softly whispers to you, "It's okay. I'm here. I love you and promise you that everything is going to be alright. Just stay here in My arms. I'll take care of you." Nothing in life provides a greater sense of peace in the face of personal sorrow than knowing that we are being held in a never-ending heavenly hug. In his arms, we find a "peace that passes understanding."

In a hymn he wrote in 1876, George Robinson said:

> Things that once were wild alarms
>   cannot now disturb my rest;
> Closed in everlasting arms,
>   pillowed on the loving breast.
> O to lie forever here,
>   doubt and care and self resign,
> While He whispers in my ear,
>   I am His, and He is mine.
> While He whispers in my ear,
>   I am His and He is mine.

Jesus knows about your troubles. Perhaps it's time for you to stop trying to figure out the *why* of your circumstances and recognize the *who* behind every situation of your life. Maybe answers will come to you at some point in life. Maybe they won't. What really matters is not that you understand, but that you trust.

God is for you. He loves you enough that He is going to allow whatever circumstances are necessary to bring the greatest good to you and the greatest glory to Himself.

The strand that completes the cord of truth about suffering in your life is that He wants to hold you in His arms and go through your struggles with you.

When my four children were small, occasionally the electricity would go off in our home at night. If they were still awake, I would hear a unified chorus cry out, "Daddy!" Melanie and I would walk through the dark rooms and collect them one by one and bring them back to our bed, where we would lie down with them. With all six of us in one bed, we would put our arms around the children and assure them that we were with them. Without fail, in a short time they would all fall asleep, secure in the fact that we were there, holding them in the dark.

You can be confident of that same fact. Your heavenly Father has you in His arms. He is with you when you are in the dark. Feel His love and know that He cares for you (see 1 Peter 5:7). Be assured that, although it may be pitch black around you right now, the sun will shine again. Until then, just rest in *Abba's* arms, knowing that He will never let you go.

Dear Father,
Thank You that in every dark moment of my life, You are present. I affirm now my trust in You even when I cannot understand Your ways. I know that nothing can separate me from Your love. Use the painful circumstances of my life to reveal more fully to me Who You are in me and who I am in You. I love and trust You, Father.

G.R.A.C.E. Group Questions

1. How can the actions of terrorists in the world today be understood in light of the teaching of the Bible about God being a loving God? Find three national tragedies in the Bible and answer these questions: How did God act in the midst of the crisis? What was the people's response? What similarities can be seen between their national crisis and those we witness in the world today?

2. Identify five New Testament Bible verses which speak to the subject of suffering. What are some of the reasons the Bible lists for suffering? How are Christians to respond to personal suffering? Show verses to prove your answer.

3. What was the last painful event you experienced in your life? How did you respond? Would you respond differently today, and if so, how?

4. What is "the revelation of His glory" that Peter mentions in 1 Peter 4:12-13? In what way might suffering be a tool to lead to this revelation?

5. How would you have tried to minister to Fred, whose wife died suddenly? What are helpful ways to minister to people who are suffering? Identify three people who suffered in the Bible and explain how others ministered to them.

6. Pause now, and pray for those in your group who are hurting. Ask them if there are other ways you can help them in addition to your prayers.

5

The Silenced Cry

FROM THE MOMENT A CHILD IS BORN, he begins to cry. Doctors say that the physical act of crying clears mucus from his airway and causes his lungs to expand. That may be the physiological reason for his cry, but what is the psychological reason for a baby's cry? What *motivates* him to cry out as if, from the moment he is born, there is an intense need that he insists be met?

Perhaps the answer to why a baby cries can best be determined by identifying what causes him to *stop* crying. The single most effective remedy for a baby's cry is to cradle him in the arms of his mother. Nurtured at her bosom, an otherwise hysterical baby will drift off into a peaceful sleep. One might conclude that babies come into the world screaming for loving intimacy. The gentle expression of intimacy from a loving parent quells the emotional storm and soothes a baby in a way nothing else can do. Watch a crying newborn as his mother takes him into her arms, speaks softly to him, and cuddles him. The result is universal.

Our Hunger for Love

There is a sense in which that baby's cry for affectionate love will continue throughout life. By the time he reaches adolescence, the child begins to look to friends to validate his value as a person and to cause him to feel loved. During the teen years, the hunger for love explodes like fireworks, often straining in every direction in an attempt to be filled. The hunger to be accepted may take on the form of an extreme fashion statement or a shared affinity with his peers for the "wild music" of his day. It may be something as simple as using the popular lingo of his generation, always an amusing and puzzling practice to the older generation, despite the fact that *their* parents thought the same things about *them*. Over the years, what was "the cat's meow" became "cool," then "groovy," then "bad," and today, "phat"—none of which offer a better substitute for the old-fashioned word, "good." But that's not the point. The bottom line is that people have a "default setting" that causes them to do or say whatever it takes to meet their basic needs for love, acceptance, and value.

Don't think for a moment that this cry for love ends when a person "grows up." No sane man today would be caught wearing a leisure suit, but 30 years ago you weren't fashionably approved if you wore otherwise. One modern dad told his young son, "In my day, we wore our baseball cap with the bill of the cap on the front of our head."

"You wore it *backwards?*" the puzzled little boy replied. The truth is that in every generation, people will do whatever it takes.

A young adult longs for intimacy and may even seek to find it through a promiscuous lifestyle. Dating services flourish as men and women search for a meaningful relationship with that special person of the opposite sex. Their dream is to find that *right* person who will make them feel loved, valued, and accepted unconditionally for the rest of their life.

The hunger to feel loved never stops. When a baby is born, when as a small child he begs for his first popular toy, and even when he is an old man driving a big, luxurious car and trying to catch "the early bird special" at the old folk's cafeteria, he wants to find a place where he is loved, valued, and accepted. The needs are normal. In fact, they are universal.

These three needs—to be loved, valued, and accepted—are intrinsic in every human being from the cradle to the coffin. If they aren't learned behavior, but are inherent to human nature from the time we are born, then why did God create man that way? Simply put, it is so that He could be the One to meet those needs. It's as though humans possess a three-pronged electrical socket within us that can only be satisfied when the life of Jesus Christ is plugged into us. Apart from Him, nothing else can ever satisfy that longing, and we will always be unfulfilled, never escaping the gnawing sense that something eternally important is missing in our lives.

Brennan Manning describes "the imposter" who lives inside each of us, vying for attention, affection, and acceptance. He writes:

> Imposters are preoccupied with acceptance and approval. Because of their suffocating need to please others, they cannot say no with the same confidence with which they say yes. And so they overextend themselves in people, projects, and causes, motivated not by personal commitment but by the fear of not living up to others' expectations.[1]

While reading the honest acknowledgment of Manning's own resident imposter, I began to wonder what the imposter who lives inside me really looks like. As I prayed, the Lord began to show him to me, and as He did,

I responded to God's voice by writing the following prayer in my personal journal:

> I, too, know that an imposter hides inside the real me. Nobody else knows him. He conceals himself so well that I only get a glimpse of him at times myself. Yet he is there nonetheless, hiding in the shadow of my consciousness, affecting the way I live and preventing me from fully knowing You to the degree that You want me to know You and that I want to know You.
>
> He is a person who is afraid, and therefore, must be in control. He demands perfection of himself and is often tense because he can't reach it, so he sedates himself with busyness—with noise and activity, sometimes even with ministry. He cares far too much about what other people think.
>
> He sometimes whispers in the recesses of my mind, describing to me a future without Your blessing and guidance. He tries to scare me by causing me to imagine worst-case scenarios about my ministry, my health, my family, my finances. His motivation isn't sinister. He's just scared and needs to understand the depths of God's love for him.

Relationship Is Everything

Ideally, life begins with a person being born into a home where he will be nurtured by loving parents and ends with one lifelong mate gently holding the hand of the other when the last breath is drawn. Between these starting and ending relationships are numerous others, each of which is intended to convey something of the relationship believers share with God.

Every good aspect of every relationship you will ever have in this world stands as a divine witness. Whatever good you have ever found in *any* relationship has been a living picture of God's love for you, drawn by His creative, artistic hand. This is why the enemy tries to destroy our relationships. He understands, better than we do, that human relationships are a display case intended to reveal the many facets of the relationship that God wants to have with us. No single human relationship can do it justice. It is the composite good in *all* of them that gives a glimpse of the believer's relationship to God through Christ Jesus. Consider how God's relationship to you is proclaimed through the human relationships He has established.

God as Our Father

Jesus referred to God as "Father" 182 times in the gospels; it is by far God's most common title of relationship in the New Testament. The word resonates with implications of loving protection and provision. Since the dawn of mankind, fatherhood has been associated with loving strength and supply. In the presence of their loving father, children feel safe. When a small child is threatened or feels afraid, the natural instinct of his heart is to cry out "Daddy!" One Bible dictionary defines a father as "the author or beginner of anything" and suggests that the word is "a title of respect for a chief, ruler, or elder."[2]

The realization that God is our heavenly Father is a source of comfort to many people. If you grew up in a home where your father loved you unconditionally, expressed affection and affirmation, and gave gentle guidance and encouragement for you to be your best in every situation, then you already have a healthy mental matrix upon which your concept of God as Father can be built. A child's first impression of God is shaped by the way he perceives his own earthly father. He will often carry that underlying concept of God with him throughout life.

However, not everybody grew up in a home where there was a loving father. One man said to me, "In your teaching today, you talked about understanding our heavenly Father's love and acceptance for us, but that's hard for me. My father was never anything other than harsh and judgmental toward me." His point is well taken. Some people grew up with an overbearing, authoritarian father, one who demanded nothing less than perfection from his children. Rewards were few, but punishment for failing to meet his standards came quickly. Others grew up in a house with an absentee dad whose lack of involvement communicated a lack of concern.

God *may* be like your father, but it is also important to understand that God may be *nothing* like your earthly father. If you grew up in an environment that now causes the word "father" to evoke a negative response in your mind or emotions, it will be important to educate yourself about the fatherhood of God. What kind of Father is God?

Phillip once said to Jesus, "Show us the Father, and it is enough for us." His request implied that he wanted to know what kind of Person God is. "Let us see Him," he said. "Then we will know and be satisfied."

Jesus responded by saying to Phillip, "he who has seen me has seen the Father" (John 14:9). If you want to know what kind of Father God is, look at Jesus. Consider how He related to those He loved.

- ◆ He loved them unconditionally (see John 13:1).

- ◆ He was patient with their weaknesses (see Matthew 8:25-26).

- ◆ He hurt when they hurt (see John 11:33-35).

- ◆ He equipped them to do anything He asked them to do (see Matthew 28:17-20).

- ◆ He promised to *never* leave or forsake them (see Matthew 28:20; Hebrews 13:5).

Do you get the picture of the kind of heavenly Father you have? Jesus said, "I and the Father are one" (John 10:30). Some people imagine God to be the harsh, judgmental Person in the Trinity and that Jesus is the "go-between" who calms God down on our behalf. However, the attitude of God is exactly the same as that of Jesus. He adores you and has committed Himself to you for all eternity.

If you struggle with seeing God as a loving Father, it may be helpful for you to read the gospels *slowly*, pausing and writing down every positive quality you read about the kind of Father He really is. Nothing robs believers of joy like a faulty concept of God.[3] As long as one believes that God is critiquing his every move, he will never feel free to relax and enjoy life. When we come to understand, however, that God laughs with delight every time He looks at us (see Zephaniah 3:17), we become like the little child who cries out, "Daddy, watch this! Watch this!" Your Daddy (*Abba*) is watching you, and He is thrilled with what He sees!

God as Our Mother

It was a difficult journey for me to begin to view God acting not only as my heavenly Father, but also as a Mother. I had a cultural hurdle to overcome. The very idea of God acting as a Mother evoked thoughts of liberal seminaries whose commitment to feminist theology was well-known. Having been reared in a solidly conservative tradition, I cringed to think about God in a maternal way. I had heard about those who used feminine pronouns when speaking of God, and I didn't like it.

My perception was that they insisted on using the feminine pronoun when they referred to God not because they wanted to express intimacy with Him, but rather because they were promoting an egalitarian approach to theology which served their own political agenda.

However, I have come to see that God indeed does relate to His children in maternal ways as well as paternal. In the Bible, God clearly presents Himself relating to His children in a motherly role.

Consider God's words in Isaiah 66:12-13:

> And you will be nursed, you will be carried on the hip and fondled on the knees. As one whom his mother comforts, so will I comfort you.

God promises that when His children need comfort, He will pick us up and hold us on His hip like a mother tends to her restless baby. He will put us on his knees, play with us, gently love us, and talk to us until we are comforted.

In another verse comparing Himself to a mother, God says:

> Can a woman forget her nursing child and have no compassion on the son of her womb? Even these may forget, but I will not forget you (Isaiah 49:15).

"Will a new mother abandon her nursing child?" God asks. "It's unlikely, but even if she would, I would never do that to you." It's not uncommon for fathers to walk out on their babies. Mothers seldom do, and God *never* will.

Most of all, God is like a perfect mother because He is our Comforter. His gentleness soothes the hurting Christian. The Psalmist understood the motherly aspect of God when he said, "Surely I have composed and quieted my soul; like a weaned child rests against his mother" (Psalm 131:2).

When I was a small child, there was a particular practice my mother did that had an immediate effect on me. Maybe it would be after I had been hurt and was crying. Perhaps it would be at times when she was simply expressing affection to me. There were probably many different situations in which it might happen, but the experience was almost transcendent for the little boy I remember. It caused me to feel at rest in a way that few things in life have ever done.

My mother would gently stroke my hair. It was that simple. I don't remember what she said at those times. I can't even clearly describe the surrounding circumstances at any of the times she did it. I just remember her doing it—stroking my hair gently. What does stand out in my mind is how I felt in those moments. I *felt* love from my mother. I felt safe, accepted, *comforted*. Regardless of the circumstances, I felt like everything was going to be okay.

Maybe that habit comes with motherhood. I've seen Melanie do the same with our children and even noticed our daughter doing it to my grandchildren. It is a simple maternal expression of love that speaks volumes to a child.

Dads don't typically comfort their children in that same way, and even when they do, it doesn't have the same effect as the loving comfort of a mother. When my children were very small and would get hurt, they would run *past* me, crying in an urgent rush for their mother. I understood. I was a kid once too. Sometimes, only a mother will do.

You may find your concept of God is strengthened in a way that brings a deeper sense of intimacy into your relationship with Him if you begin to think of the maternal aspects of His affections toward you. Perhaps you are completely comfortable with approaching Him as a Mother. Maybe, however, you find the idea of God acting as a Mother to be uncomfortable due to the traditions in which you were reared.

Spiritual growth often requires that we choose to rise above the traditions which have influenced our lives. At times in our journey of grace, it is necessary to embrace what the Bible teaches and what the Holy Spirit shows us even though it may be uncomfortable initially. I'm not trying to cause a doctrinal shift in your mind about God and gender. In fact, God is Spirit and therefore without gender.

What I *am* trying to do is to encourage you to allow the Holy Spirit to broaden your understanding of God's role in your life so that you will know the benefit of motherly love in your relationship with Him. Intimacy between a mother and child is a particular kind of experience unlike any other love relationship we will ever know. If you want to fully understand God's love for you, it is important to know His fatherly *and* motherly qualities. It takes both to fully reveal who He is to us.

God as Our Friend

The French poet, Jacques Delille wrote, "Fate chooses your relations, you choose your friends." None of us decided into which family we would be born, but we do decide who we want to be our friends. Nobody wants to be best friends with every person he meets. However, there are certain people who come across our paths whom we decide we would like to know better. We make the effort to establish a relationship with them, and over a period of time, deep friendships develop.

My friend Debbie shared an amazing experience with me not long ago. She was a junior in high school during the time that Richard Nixon was President of the United States. In one of her classes, she had an assignment to write a report on the President's wife, Pat Nixon. As she studied Mrs. Nixon's life, Debbie gained a deep respect and appreciation for her.

One of the coincidental details of Mrs. Nixon's life that Debbie learned was that they both had the same birthday. She decided to write the first lady and express her respect and appreciation for her. In her letter, she made her aware that they both shared the same birthday.

A short time later Debbie received a letter from Mrs. Nixon—not a form letter, but a personal, handwritten letter. Debbie decided to respond to Mrs. Nixon's letter by writing her a second time. She did, and again Mrs. Nixon responded with a personal letter. The result was that the 17-year-old high school girl and the President's wife became pen pals. Debbie and Mrs. Nixon wrote each other for several years.

In March of 1974, the Nixons were invited to the opening of The Grand Ole Opry in Nashville, Tennessee. The opening day also happened to coincide with Mrs. Nixon's and Debbie's birthday. To her delight and surprise, the now 19-year-old Debbie received a letter from Mrs. Nixon, inviting her to be her guest at The Grand Ole Opry. Debbie went to Nashville, where she stood waiting with visiting dignitaries to meet President and Mrs. Nixon. One snobbish woman looked this young 19-year-old girl up and down and arrogantly asked, "And why are *you* here?"

Debbie simply answered, "I'm an invited guest of Mrs. Nixon."

As Debbie told the story to me, she said, "I couldn't believe it. There I was as the *guest* of the guest of honor." Among all those who clamored to have a brief moment with Mrs. Nixon, 19-year-old Debbie Childers was her guest and her friend.

It's an amazing facet of the gospel of grace that God has chosen you to be His friend.

You aren't God's friend in the same sense that Mrs. Nixon and Debbie were friends. Theirs was a casual connection, but God's connection to you is very personal and deeply intimate. His desire is that the friendship you two share will be the closest relationship you will ever experience.

Friends Know Each Other Intimately

One benefit of an intimate friendship is that there is nothing that can't be shared between them. True friendship doesn't disconnect because of faults each person may have. Ralph Waldo Emerson said, "It is one of the blessings of old friends that you can afford to be stupid with them."

God is that kind of friend to you. Do you feel free to share the deepest and darkest aspects of your life with Him? You can because He is completely accepting of you. Understanding and believing in God's complete acceptance is a vital key in developing intimacy with him.

Five couples sat together one evening in our home. We had been singing choruses, laughing, talking, and sharing the snacks each couple had brought. As the time approached for us to pray together, one of the ladies in the group began to speak. Tears filled her eyes and her voice quivered as she said, "John (not his real name) and I need your prayers. We agreed before we arrived tonight that we would ask you to pray for us concerning a problem we have." She then began to explain that she had committed adultery and had recently confessed her sin to her husband. Tears streamed down the cheeks of both of them. Those of us in the room began to cry too as Mary (not her real name) described what had happened and the impact it had on their relationship.

After she had finished talking, my wife, Melanie, spoke first. "Mary," she said, "the first thing you need to know is that there is nothing you could ever tell us that would cause us to love you any less." As Melanie spoke, I am sure that everybody in the room felt what I felt—the manifest presence of God. When she ministered loving acceptance to our friend, we were all aware of Jesus speaking through her at that moment. His gracious acceptance and gentle Spirit permeated the room.

We had John and Mary move their chairs to the center of the room, where we all gathered around them, and one by one, prayed for them. We then hugged them, held them, and assured them of our love. The healing had begun.

Intimacy requires openness. You don't have to put your best foot forward with God. He *knows* you—*everything* about you—and still loves you completely. There is nothing you could ever tell Him that would cause Him to love or accept you any less. The familiar quote is true: "A friend is someone who knows everything about you and totally accepts you as you are." "The Lord's lovingkindnesses indeed never cease, For His compassions never fail. They are new every morning. *Great* is [His] faithfulness" (Lamentations 2:22-23, emphasis added). You'll never have another friend like God.

Understanding God's total acceptance not only frees us from the prison of self-condemnation, but also empowers us to love others who have sinned. We are able to give them the same compassionate tenderness of Jesus that we ourselves have received. Those who don't know they have received compassion can't give it. It is natural for the one who has experienced the gentle acceptance of Jesus to tenderly share it with others.

Lorraine Hansberry wrote *A Raisin In The Sun*, the story of an African-American man who makes mistakes that shatter his family's hopes and dreams. When he confesses to his family and asks for their forgiveness, his sister responds in hostile anger, calling him horrible names.

Her mother interrupts her display and says, "I thought I taught you to love him." "Love him? There is nothing left to love," the sister responds in anger. Then the mother answers:

> There is always something left to love. And if you ain't learned that, you ain't learned nothing. Have you cried for that boy today? I don't mean for yourself and for the family 'cause we lost the money. I mean for him; what he's been through and what it done to him. Child, when do you think is the time to love somebody the most; when they done good

> and made things easy for everybody? Well, then, you ain't through learning—because that ain't the time at all. It's when he's at his lowest and can't believe in hisself 'cause the world done whipped him so. When you starts measuring somebody, measure him right child, measure him right. Make sure you done taken into account what hills and valleys he come through before he got to wherever he is.

God has seen the hills and valleys of your life. He has seen you at your best and your worst, and yet still loves you unconditionally. He wants you to share yourself completely with Him with complete confidence that He will not respond in criticism. The score card on your life was torn up at the cross, and God has stopped keeping score on you. Your friendship with Him isn't about how you behave. Ironically, the realization of that fact is the only thing that *will* cause your behavior to change. Friendship with God is about enjoying each other's company. It is a union which will never end for all eternity. He wants you to tell Him everything, and He will do the same.

Jesus said, "I have called you friends, for all things that I have heard from my Father I have made known to you" (John 15:15). As you walk with Him, He will reveal more and more to you about the Father until the day you see Him face to face. He is the "friend who sticks closer than a brother" (Proverbs 18:24). Emily Dickinson once said, "My friends are my estate." That's how Jesus feels toward you. You are His inheritance, a gift from God to Him. Four times in the Gospel of John, Jesus refers to believers as those whom God has given Him.[4]

Enjoy the Relationship

Empty religion focuses on laws, but understanding that God's love is like that of a strong father, a nurturing mother, and a faithful friend can cause you to finally relax and rest in the relationship you have with Him. As a baby you came into the world crying for love, but now you can hear the voice of the Holy Spirit saying, "Hush now, child. Dry your inner tears. God loves you! He loves you with a love that is too big for boundaries. It's a love that will never die." God, alone, can silence your cry for love. All you have to do is believe Him and receive His love, then spend all eternity simply resting and reveling in Him.

Dear Father,
Your love is more deep and wide than I could ever fully know in this life. May the Holy Spirit show me the specific times in my life each day that You act toward me like a loving Father, a gentle Mother, and a dear Friend. Expand my understanding of Your love, and in response to that Divine love, may my own heart grow more in love with You each day.

G.R.A.C.E. Group Questions

1. This chapter mentions three main needs that every person possesses. What are they? What are some ways that people try to meet these three needs at church? At work? At home? With friends?

2. What adjectives would you use to describe your earthly father? In what way did he exhibit the characteristics of God? Identify three verses that reveal characteristics of God as a Father.

3. Is there an "imposter" who lives within you? In what ways does he interfere with your relationship to God?

4. Read Psalm 131:2; Isaiah 49:14-15; 66:12-13. Discuss the way these verses relate to Christians today. Describe a time in your own life when God acted toward you like a mother would respond to her children.

5. List five important characteristics of a true friend, in order of importance to you. How have you seen God demonstrate these qualities in your relationship with Him?

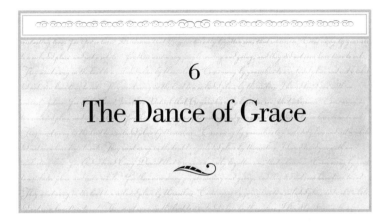

6

The Dance of Grace

It was December, and I was in the Chinese countryside, three hours outside Beijing. Temperatures were hovering around ten below zero. I could see my own breath in the cold air of the unheated storage room in the abandoned factory where I both slept and taught the Bible during my time in this poverty-stricken community.

Fifteen people sat around me in a circle, having sneaked into the room one at a time in order to avoid detection by the police. "Aren't you afraid of going to jail?" one of the believers asked me.

"Are you?" I asked. It's illegal for Christians in China to meet together as we were doing and we all knew that. However, these believers were so hungry for Bible teaching that they would risk their very lives to attend this Bible study.

I had taught for 13 hours that day. Now it was the evening, and we were praying and worshiping God. These brave Christians had been singing Chinese hymns, offering praise to my God and theirs for His goodness.

There was a lull in the room as we were all praying silently, when an 87-year-old woman began to sing alone.

I had spoken to her earlier through my translator and knew her personal story. She and her husband had been separated during a war in China more than 30 years earlier. As Japanese and Chinese soldiers fought all around her, she hid in the corner of a building. Friends around her were being killed, but the soldiers all brushed past her, seeming not to notice she was there.

Finally the shooting stopped, and the soldiers all left. She said that her immediate thought was, *There must be a God because there is no other explanation for why I survived what just happened. I want to know this God.* Ten years passed before she heard about an underground church service near where she lived. Taking her daughter by the hand, she said, "Let's go to this church where we can meet this God who spared my life ten years ago." They went to the house church that day, and there she met Jesus Christ.

Now here I was, 20 years later, sitting in an abandoned factory where one family had secretly taken up residence. I had been teaching about intimacy with Christ, but this 87-year-old lady was about to make the lesson I taught even more real to me. She closed her eyes and began to sing.

It was a soft and sweet-sounding song in the Mandarin language. As she sang, tears began to stream down her wrinkled cheeks and over her radiant smile. I couldn't understand the words she sang, but I was aware that she was literally exuding the love of Jesus Christ. Suddenly, I sensed the manifest presence of God in a powerful way.

I couldn't hold back my tears, and as I looked around the room, I saw the others were crying too. I looked back at this saint who now appeared to be in a world of her own, seemingly oblivious to our presence. It was obvious—she was not singing for us. She was singing to Jesus.

In a few moments, she finished her song and a holy hush lingered in the room. She paused for a moment and then opened her eyes and looked at me. "Every day *He* is looking forward to my coming," she said with wet cheeks and an angelic smile. I felt like a little boy who was being taught a lesson he had never heard. Looking through teary eyes, I smiled and simply nodded.

Our Honeymoon Home

"He is looking forward to my coming." Have you ever thought of that? Most people think about how happy we will be to see Jesus Christ face to face, but have you considered how anxious He is to see you? Christians are called the bride of Christ in the New Testament. One day He will come again, and those of us who are His bride will be united with Him in an eternal marriage. Jesus said,

> I go to prepare a place for you. If I go and prepare a place for you, I will come again and receive you unto Myself; that where I am, there you may be also (John 14:2-3).

In the last chapter, you were asked to consider your relationship to God as your father, mother, and friend. However, the most intimate relationship by which we are identified with Christ is that of a bride. One day we will hear a resounding invitation echoing through the universe, "The Bridegroom is coming! Come out to meet Him" (see Matthew 25:6). In that moment, every Christian will see the One whose passion for them was so great that He thought it better to die for them than to live without them.

Better than Cinderella

You are familiar with the tale of Cinderella and how a handsome prince fell in love with her and changed her identity from a poor servant girl to a princess. Your own story causes hers to pale by comparison. Unlike the story of Cinderella, yours is *true*. The unabridged version of your story is told throughout the New Testament, but a short preview of how you have been rescued by your own Prince Charming is told in Ezekiel 16, in a parallel description of God's history with His people in Jerusalem. He begins with a portrayal of what you were like when He found you. Cinderella's humble beginnings were nothing by comparison to your own. God says:

> Your origin and your birth are from the land of the Canaanite, your father was an Amorite and your mother a Hittite. As for your birth, on the day you were born your navel cord was not cut, nor were you washed with water for cleansing; you were not rubbed with salt or even wrapped with cloths. No eye looked with pity on you to do any of these things for you, to have compassion on you. Rather you were thrown out into the open field, for you were abhorred on the day you were born (Ezekiel 16:3-5).

This is a description of a person who came into the world destined for disaster from the start. "Your father was an Amorite and your mother was a Hittite." The tone of the statement even sounds like an indictment, doesn't it? Indeed, it does point to a sordid ancestral past. The Amorites were a branch of Canaanite giants, steeped in idolatry and rebellion against God (see Amos 2:9). The depravity of the Hittites was so great that they were even known for their involvement in bestiality.[1] "Don't think for a moment that you were born with some inherent good in you that caught my attention," God is saying to unfaithful Jerusalem.

So it is with us. We came into the world from a spiritual family line which opposed God every step of the way. Born in Adam, there was nothing at all spiritually attractive about us. Unbelievers flatter themselves by thinking they possess any redeeming spiritual quality. On his very best behavior, man's righteousness still looks disgusting in the sight of God (see Isaiah 64:6).

During one meal I was served on a visit to a rural part of China, my hostess was about to drop a variety of chicken parts into my bowl of noodles. The problem with the parts was they were all from the *inside* of the chicken—internal organs and mystery meat that Americans generally wouldn't consider eating. As she reached across with the chopsticks holding something from the serving bowl that I neither recognized nor wanted to put in my mouth, she paused and looked at me as if to ask, "Would you like some?" I politely shook my head, indicating no. Immediately she put those parts back into the serving bowl, dug a little deeper, and without hesitation reached over and dropped a chicken *foot* on top of my bowl of noodles! (Maybe it *is* called a claw, but it was a *foot* to me). She beamed a bright smile at me as if she had just uncovered a hidden treasure in the bowl of food. I feebly smiled back at her, took a deep breath and began to eat the noodles, wondering how I was going to smuggle that chicken foot out of the room so that she would never know I didn't eat it.

When unredeemed man offers up his best to God, it turns His stomach. Even an unbeliever's best *religious* effort is no more of an improvement than was my chicken foot. Whether we were religious or not, at best we were lying in our own filth when God first came to us.

The Gift of Life

Continuing with His narrative about how He saved His people, God said,

> When I passed by you and saw you squirming in your blood, I said to you while you were in your blood, "Live!" Yes, I said to you while you were in your blood, "Live!" (Ezekiel 16:6).

The first and foundational action that God took in bringing you to Himself was to declare to you, "Live!" Many modern Christians believe that the most important thing in salvation is that our sins are forgiven, but as strange as it may seem, forgiveness is actually a secondary matter. The primary element of salvation is that we have received divine *life*. It was necessary for God to forgive us, but He gave us life so that He could accomplish His main purpose—taking up residence in us so that we might live in union with Him for all eternity.

Regeneration is the quickening of a dead spirit, a spirit filled with sin, which at salvation becomes supernaturally made alive by the divine work of God. There was nothing about you that wanted God before you were a Christian. Nobody naturally seeks to know God (see Romans 3:11). However, despite the fact that you didn't want God, He wanted you! For that reason, He sent the Holy Spirit to draw you to Himself with an irresistible love.

Forgiveness of sins is a tremendous aspect of salvation, but equating Christianity and forgiveness has produced a generation of modern Christians who know they are going to heaven and are now simply waiting for it to happen. Their faith is defined primarily in terms of what *has* happened and what *will* happen. "My sins have been forgiven, and I am going to heaven," they reason.

What about the meantime? Where is the *abundant* life Jesus promised (see John 10:10)? Authentic Christianity is not so much a transaction by which a person's sins are forgiven as it is a love story between two people—*you* and *Jesus Christ*. Do you daily personalize the redemption story, or do you simply see yourself as one in a great mass of people whose sins have been forgiven and who are one day going to heaven? Intimacy with Christ is only possible when we routinely personalize His love for us.

The Dance

He entered into the room, which was filled with noise and activity. There was music, laughter, and talking. His eyes scanned the room, searching for that one whose very face caused his breath to quicken and his heart rate to increase. He loved her, yet it was more than that. He *wanted* her. He wanted her to be his, and not just tonight, but forever.

Then he saw her. Across the crowded room, she stood—as if she had been unknowingly waiting for him all her life. She was beautiful. No, not beautiful—she was *stunning*. "God, I must have her!" every fiber of his being resonated. "I want to spend my life with her. I want to love her and cherish her and hold her. I want to take care of her and spoil her."

He walked across the room, never taking his eyes off her for even a moment. The room was filled with people, but his eyes were on her alone. As he approached her, his presence caught her attention and she looked upward into his penetrating eyes. This was the moment he had been waiting for, the time he had longed for as long as he could remember. Gently and lovingly he spoke: "Would you care to dance?"

The description I have given is a true story. The two did begin to dance that day and they have never stopped. He asked her to marry him and she said yes. His plan is to do exactly what he intended from the beginning—to share his life with her and to love her so much that she will never regret the day she met him.

Not only is the story true, but you actually know the people involved. The one He desired to have so much is *you*. The Person who wanted you so badly is Jesus Christ. One day He walked into the room of this world to find *you*. He was captivated by you and determined that He would make you His own. He knew in His heart that He *must* have you, that He wouldn't live without you.

If you doubt my words about His love, read the following marriage proposal that He wrote you. These aren't my words, but His, copied here word for word exactly as He wrote them to you:

> How beautiful you are, my darling. How beautiful you are! There is no blemish in you! Arise, my darling, my beautiful one, And come along. You have made my heart beat faster with a single glance of your eyes. How delightful you are, My love, with all your charms!

This note to you is recorded in the Bible, in the Song of Solomon.[2] This book of the Bible is a love story about you and Jesus. Its words are sometimes so graphic, so intense, that throughout church history there have been those who have argued that it shouldn't even be in the Bible. However, your Divine Lover has made sure it is there. The Song of Solomon is a love poem written for you. Its eight stanzas call you beautiful no less than 15 times!

Lady Julian of Norwich was allowed to see the heart of God and the glory of the gospel. Her summary of what the Lord taught her was simply, "We are his lovers."[3] Jesus is consumed with you. Speaking about you, He said, "Who is this...fair as the moon, bright as the sun, majestic as the stars?" (Song of Solomon 6:10 NIV).

You may not feel that way about yourself, but it makes no difference. What He says is an objective fact whether you believe it or not. If you don't believe it now, rest assured that you *will* believe it because He is going to keep telling you how beautiful and precious you are to Him throughout all eternity. One day, either now or later, the reality of His words will transform you.

Do you remember the day that He asked you to dance? It was the day you believed the gospel. Maybe it was in church, or perhaps it was when a friend shared his faith with you. Maybe it was when you were all alone and heard the voice of the Holy Spirit. Do you remember what you experienced then as He reached out to you? The bride in the Song of Solomon spoke for us all when she said, "My feelings were aroused for him" (5:4). That happened to us all when Jesus swept us off our feet, and we trusted Him.

Don't think it irreverent to view Christ in a romantic way. He is the One who calls us His bride. He is the One who wrote to us in terms of passion and romance. We simply *respond* to Him. "We love Him because He first loved us" (1 John 4:19 NKJV). We didn't initiate or set the pace for this relationship; He did. We have simply responded to His irresistible charm, affirming by faith, "My beloved is mine, and I am His" (Song of Solomon 2:16). Like every new bride, our profession of faith in Him is nothing less than the thrilling realization that, "I am my beloved's, and his desire is for *me*" (7:10, emphasis added).

I didn't dream up the idea of the dance as a literary metaphor to describe your relationship to Him. That is how *He* described it. In Zephaniah 3:17, the Bible says, "He will *exult* over you with joy" (emphasis added). *Strong's Concordance* defines the word "exult" (sometimes translated "rejoice") in the following way: "To spin around under the influence of a violent emotion."

One character quipped, "I grew up in a church so strict we were taught that premarital sex was wrong because it might (horrors!) lead to *dancing,* and now you tell me that the Lord dances over me?" It's true, He does. The love of Jesus Christ for you is not just a "gentle Jesus, meek and mild" kind of love. It is a love filled with passion. It is a love that caused your Prince Charming to wield His sword (of the Spirit) and fight the dragon (the devil, see Revelation 12:9) for you!

His love for you is great! One might say that the love of Jesus for you could be X-rated, not because of impurity, but because of *intensity.* Does that idea make you feel uncomfortable? It shouldn't; He really does love you with an intensity beyond human comprehension. You are the pearl of great price for which He paid everything He owned to possess (see Matthew 13:45-46). Don't be afraid of an intense love from Him. His love is intense, but His ways are gentle.

Cheryl's Story

A young woman named Cheryl learned about God's intense love for her after a season of adversity. Cheryl was a typical young mother who had been married for four years. She and Lee's life together had seemed fairly normal early in their marriage, but then things began to change. Lee began to act distant toward her. She attempted to find out what the problem was, but Lee only became increasingly cold as time passed. The day finally came when, to her utter disbelief, Lee packed his bags, emptied the bank account, and drove away in the only car they owned, leaving Cheryl and their two-year-old son with nothing.

A few weeks after her husband abandoned her, Cheryl discovered that Lee had been having a homosexual affair with his employer. To her shock and horror, she learned that her husband had made the decision to live an openly gay lifestyle. The weight of her burden was overwhelming. The next time Cheryl would see or hear from Lee would be seven years later as he lay dying from AIDS in a hospital bed.

She became bitter toward God in the days that followed, viewing Him as an Enemy who, for reasons beyond her comprehension, was out to get her. The darkness of depression intensified until she finally found herself one night sitting alone with a bottle of pills in her hand. But the outcome of that night was like nothing Cheryl expected. She describes the scene:

> I had self-talked my way into a state of hopelessness and despair to a point of wanting to take my own life. One evening as I sat in a dark room with pills in hand, ready to end all of the hurt, the God who I had considered my "Enemy" quietly and gently reached out to me in love. I began hearing a soft voice in my mind that kept telling me to read Philippians 4:1. Finally, I got up out of my chair, found a Bible, and read this verse: *[My beloved,] I love you and I long to see you, for you are my joy and my reward for my work. My beloved...stay true to the Lord.* God was speaking to me, and these were not the words of an enemy, but were words of love, compassion, and acceptance for me, *His beloved.*
>
> That evening I knelt and prayed a prayer of total surrender to Him. This was not a prayer for salvation, but a prayer of brokenness. It was one of absolute surrender—giving up the right to live my own way. I didn't fully comprehend all that it meant to totally surrender to Him, but somehow I knew I had to give up control of my life and allow Him to *be* my life. That evening, my "Enemy," my

> *Lord,* proclaimed His love for me and told me that
> I was *His* joy and *His* reward, and *I was His
> beloved.*[4]

In the days ahead, Jesus Christ began to teach Cheryl that He alone was her sufficiency; that He was all she really needed; in fact, that He is all *anybody* really needs.*

An Old-Fashioned Love Song

The New International Version of the Bible says that "He will rejoice over you with *singing*" (emphasis added). Can you imagine Jesus singing sweet love songs to you? The Bible says that He does. He is so enthralled because you are His that He can't keep from singing.

I was teaching from this verse one day when Helena came to me afterward and said, "I was reading that verse not long ago and noticed that it says the Lord sings over us with joy. 'Lord,' I asked, 'Do you *really* sing over me? What could you possibly sing about *me?*' Immediately," she said, "one of my favorite old songs from years gone by popped into my mind, word for word. At first I tried to dismiss it, thinking, 'This *can't* be the Lord.' But the song wouldn't stop, and shortly I knew it was indeed the Lord singing a song to *me.*"

Helena continued, "I heard Him sing to me, 'You are my sunshine, My only sunshine. You make me happy when skies are gray. You'll never know dear, how much I love you. Please don't take my sunshine away!' I realized then," Helena said, "just how much He loves me! To think that I am the sunshine of His life absolutely overwhelmed me!"

Someone might protest, "Why would the Lord sing a song to her like *that* one?" Don't think that the only songs your Prince Charming knows are religious songs. He sang the song to Helena that He knew would thrill her heart. He wasn't singing to Himself, but to her. That's how won-

---

* As a tribute to God's faithfulness through the years, Cheryl recently wrote a poem about God's divine invitation. The poem appears on page 185.

derful our Divine Lover is. He knows your favorite songs, your favorite places, your favorite *everything*. His plan is to see to it that you are able to enjoy it all—beginning now and reaching forward beyond this earth-life toward the nonexistent boundaries of eternity. Every good thing you enjoy in life is His love song to you.

My favorite place on this earth is the British Virgin Islands. All of the Caribbean is beautiful, but there is something about the beauty of these particular islands that is almost hypnotic to me. As Melanie and I vacationed there one summer, I lay in a hammock at Cane Garden Bay on Tortola, unable to keep my mind on the book I had brought to read. I stared out over the powdery, white sand across the crystal clear, blue water. As I watched sailboats on the horizon, at one point I literally felt a deep sense of joy and prayed, "God, this is *awesome*! You did a great job here!" At that moment, a thought entered my mind as a still, small voice and gently whispered, "This is nothing. Wait until you see the rest I have for you!"

He sings over you with joy! Your Prince Charming has prepared so much for you. "No eye has seen, no ear has heard, no mind has conceived what God has prepared for those who love Him—but God has revealed it to us by His Spirit" (1 Corinthians 2:9-10 NIV). Your Bridegroom sings to you every day. Listen. Can you hear the music? Spirit-filled living is nothing less than a perpetual dance with Jesus.

The background music is always there because He is always singing. Do you recognize the tune? Remember, He doesn't only know religious songs. He knows every *romantic* song and sings a thousand stanzas to you everyday—in the laughter of children, in the beauty of a sunset, in the music that stirs you, in the flavor of your favorite food, in the intimacy of your marriage. He knows *your* favorite song.

In her poem "Aurora Leigh," Elizabeth Barrett Browning wrote:

> Earth's crammed with heaven,
> And every common bush afire with God;
> But only he who sees, takes off his shoes,
> The rest sit round it and pluck blackberries.

The song of God's love for you resonates through the universe. Jesus said, "He who has ears to hear, let him hear" (Matthew 11:15). When you hear the tune, do you recognize His voice singing to you? Don't waste your time plucking blackberries when the Lover of the universe is inviting you to the big dance.

The Wedding Gifts

In Ezekiel 16, God said to those He loves, "When I passed by you and saw you, I could tell that you were ready to be loved. So I spread my garment over you to cover your nakedness. Then I made a solemn oath to you, entering into a covenant with you, saying, 'You *will* be Mine!'" (paraphrase of Ezekiel 16:8). That was only the beginning.

A covenant is an irrevocable commitment which cannot be broken under any circumstance, even if the other party fails to keep their part of the agreement. God has said to you, "Regardless of what you may or may not do, I'm going to fulfill what I plan to do. Nothing will stop Me from making you Mine forever. You *will* be My love. I will do everything necessary to ensure that it happens." Consider the things described in Ezekiel 16 that the Lord has given to you, the love of His life:

♦ *He has made you spiritually clean.* "Then I bathed you with water, washed off your blood from you..." (16:9). Jesus said, "You are already clean because of the word which I have spoken to you" (John 15:3). The filth of your past is forever gone. It has been washed away by Jesus. In place of your past filth, by the abundance of His grace, you have been given the righteousness of Jesus Christ (see Romans 5:17). You are now holy (see 1 Corinthians 3:16-17) because Jesus Christ Himself has become your righteousness (see 1 Corinthians 1:30).

✦ *He has given you His Spirit.* "I...anointed you with oil" (Ezekiel 16:9). In Scripture, oil is a type of the Holy Spirit. Because Jesus loves you, He has placed His own Spirit within you to protect and guide you. No man sends the love of his life into dangerous places where she will not be protected. Jesus has promised, "I will never desert you, nor will I ever forsake you" (Hebrews 13:5).

✦ *He has given you spiritual gifts.* "I adorned you with ornaments, put bracelets on your hands and a necklace around your neck..." (Ezekiel 16:11). The New Testament affirms that when Jesus rose from the dead, He gave gifts to those He redeemed (see 1 Corinthians 12:4-11; Ephesians 4:8). You have been given spiritual gifts which equip you to live victoriously in this life.

✦ *He has transformed you into royalty.* "You were exceedingly beautiful and advanced to royalty. Then your fame went forth among the nations on account of your beauty, for it was perfect because of My splendor which I bestowed on you" (Ezekiel 16:13-14). God has given you a new identity. When you became a Christian you became a partaker of His divine nature (see 2 Peter 1:4). You are now a person of royal descent (see 1 Peter 2:9) and bear the very name of Christ.

A Fairy Tale Come True

The story of Cinderella is a fun tale for children, but it isn't real. Your story, on the other hand, is absolutely true. Jesus loves you and has committed all of His divine resources to ensure that you will be His bride forever. He has gone to prepare for the wedding and will one day come back for you to take you to your eternal honeymoon home. In the meantime, *every day He looks forward to your coming.* He loves you so very much and can barely wait for the time when you and He will live together face to face in heaven. It won't be long, so be ready.

During the late 1800s, a young girl named Florence Martus lived with her brother in a lighthouse in Savannah, Georgia. His job was to serve as caretaker of the lighthouse that led ships safely into the harbor.

One day Florence had to go into town to take care of some business. While she was there, she met a handsome, young sailor from a distant port. It was love at first sight and led to a short whirlwind romance. Knowing that he must leave, the young man quickly asked Florence to marry him. He promised to soon return to Savannah to claim his bride. Then he sailed off into the horizon.

Every day Florence stood on the bank, waiting for her love to return. She waved her apron at each ship she saw approaching the harbor, in hopes that it might be his. She held her breath in eager anticipation, hoping that each ship would be the one to bring her love back to her. Florence kept up her watchful vigil for 44 years, rain or shine. Sadly, the love of her life never returned to her.

Today on River Street, near the Savannah River, there stands a statue of Florence Martus, honoring her for never giving up hope. Florence was officially recognized as "Savannah's Sweetheart" in the 1930s and remained so until her death in 1943. As ships enter the port of Savannah today, the statue of Florence Martus greets them, still waving her apron and guiding them into the harbor.

Christians today stand on the edge of time, looking at the horizon toward the boundary between time and eternity. Sometimes, the rains are harsh, and the cold wind is bitter. However, despite what life may bring, we anxiously await our Love's return for us. Unlike the waving girl of Savannah, we won't be disappointed. One day you will see Him, and your heart will be thrilled when at last you hear Jesus say:

> Arise, my darling, my beautiful one,
> And come along.
> For behold, the winter is past,
> The rain is over and gone.
> The flowers have already appeared in the land;
> The time has arrived for pruning the vines,
> And the voice of the turtledove
>   has been heard in our land.
> The fig tree has ripened its figs
> And the vines in blossom
>   have given forth their fragrance.
> Arise, my darling, my beautiful one,
>   And come along...[5]

In that day we will meet face to face the One whom, "having not seen, you love" (1 Peter 1:8 NKJV). We will look into the eyes that have never looked away from us even once. We will be embraced by His outstretched arms and will hear His voice audibly. I'm not sure what His first words to you will be, but it wouldn't surprise me if the first thing He says as He stares deeply into your eyes is simply, "Let's dance."

*D*ear Father,
Thank You for loving me so much! With enthusiasm, I accept Your proposal to be Your bride for all eternity. Mine is a Cinderella story come true! I can hardly wait for You to return to take me to the home You and I will share for eternity. Even so, come quickly!

G.R.A.C.E. GROUP QUESTIONS

1. Jesus said that He has gone to prepare a place for you. Being specific, describe what you believe heaven will be like. What are you looking forward to most about heaven?

2. Read Ezekiel 16:6. Describe the time in your own life when the Lord came to you and you heard His voice saying, "Live!" How did He speak to you? How has your life changed since then?

3. Find other verses in the Song of Solomon, not mentioned in this chapter, which indicate how Christ feels about you. Combine the verses to form a note from Him to you.

4. What song would you want to hear Jesus sing to you? Read or recite the words to that song to the group. Why did you select that particular song? Other than songs, what are some other ways that you hear the voice of Jesus Christ singing to you?

5. Identify two spiritual gifts you believe that you have received from God. In what ways can you use those gifts for His glory?

6. Watch your favorite movie and note what stirs you. What do you find in common with the way the movie stirs you and how God stirs you?

7

From Must to Trust

SOMETIMES I HAVE WONDERED IF I'M spiritually retarded. I hear some Christians describe how God shows them the need for a change of direction in their lives, and how they immediately make a course correction. I have often envied these people, because that has seldom been my experience. God often has to repeat what He says to me through various means until I finally respond, "Oh! Lord, that's *You* talking to me!" It isn't that I want to be insensitive to His voice, I just get so preoccupied at times with doing the things I think He has given me to do, that I don't always hear Him when He speaks.

Maybe I'm not actually spiritually retarded. It may be that I have some sort of Spiritual Attention Deficit Disorder (S.A.D.D.?). Children with A.D.D. have problems filtering out the cacophony of stimuli in their surrounding environment. Consequently, it appears that they aren't paying attention to anything, when in reality they are paying attention to *everything* so that they are unable to focus on that which should have their undivided attention. That describes fairly well much of my Christian experience: I have often been distracted by many things and missed "the best part" (see Luke 10:38-42).

Remember the story in chapter one about my time at the cabin by the pond? That wasn't the first time God had spoken on the matter of my becoming too busy for the kind of intimacy with Him that He wants to share with those whom He loves. I have loved the Lord since I was a child, but it has often been on my terms and my timetable.

At times my moments of loving interaction with God have been much like the husband who occasionally gives flowers to his wife to make *himself* feel good. To be honest, at times I have sought intimacy with Him solely for my own benefit, for my pleasure. How healthy can a marriage like that be? Self-centeredness in any love relationship is at best a sign of immaturity and at worst an indication of a lack of serious commitment. There is certainly nothing to dispute in the Westminster Confession's assertion that "man's chief end is to glorify God and enjoy Him forever," but a mature person knows that the best way to find pleasure for yourself is to bring pleasure to the one you love. The point is that Christianity is not intended to be egocentric, but Christocentric.

It's About Him, Not Us

God doesn't exist for us. We exist for Him and for His pleasure (see Revelation 4:11 KJV). If we would know Him intimately, it's important to understand that He sets the terms of the relationship. Jeff Imbach notes, "This is God's life and God's purpose, a river of life within us. We did not start the flow and we will not provide the current."[1]

If you want to dance with God, you had better be prepared to let Him lead. Otherwise, you'll find yourself stepping all over your own feet. However, if you do learn to let Him lead, you'll have the dance of a lifetime to the music of His never-ending love.

In His goodness, God determines to take us to a deeper level of intimacy, to a place beyond our adolescent approach to intimacy with Him. We might still be content with the childish devotion of a little boy passing love notes in school. But God wants us to move past our superficial faith and into a much deeper love and more mature relationship with Him. If you sincerely hunger to know Him in the most intimate sense of the word,[2] He *will* take you there. The fact that you hunger to know Him deeply demonstrates that He is already moving you toward greater intimacy.

I realize now that God had been speaking to me for quite some time about impediments to intimacy with Him, showing me that His desire was to bring me greater pleasure in Him, thus fulfilling His pleasure in me. He had already spoken to me through a stress-induced rash, through my precious wife, through my loving, yet "concerned" ("Son, I worry about you") mother, and through friends who saw more clearly than I did that my frenzied pace hindered a deepening intimacy.

Richard Foster couldn't have drawn me into *A Testament of Devotion* by Quaker writer Thomas Kelly any quicker if he had hypnotized me. His promise of a supernatural life *without* jammed schedules and frenzied days looked like a spiritual oasis to me. He writes in the introduction to Kelly's book:

> Then my eyes came upon [Kelly's] words of hope and promise: "We have hints that there is a way of life vastly richer and deeper than all this hurried existence, a life of unhurried serenity and peace and power. If only we could slip over into that Center!"

> Instinctively, I knew that he was speaking of a reality beyond my experience. Please understand me, I was not ungodly or irreverent—just the opposite. My problem was that I was so serious, so concerned to do what was right, that I felt compelled to respond to every call of service. After all, there were wonderful opportunities to minister in Christ's name. The end result, however, was what Kelly described as "an intolerable scramble of panting feverishness."[3]

I can certainly relate to Foster's and Kelly's dilemma, and I am convinced that many evangelical Christians today find themselves in the same place—sincerely serving the Lord from a heart of love, but trying to do so much so quickly that they miss the depths of intimacy He longs to share with them. "Panting feverishness," Kelly called it. That might be an accurate slogan for many modern churches. The sad part of it is that some Christians would view it as a *positive* slogan for the church.

One morning, I read the prayer that Jesus prayed on the night before He was to be crucified. He said, "I glorified You on the earth, having accomplished the work which You have given Me to do" (John 17:4). For some reason that didn't make sense to me, my eyes filled with tears as I read that verse. I prayed, "Father, that's what I want to be able to say to You when I'm facing my hour of death. 'I have glorified You on this earth. I have accomplished what You gave me to do.'"

The intent of my prayer was to express the desire to leave nothing undone that God wants me to *do* during my lifetime. From my childhood, my paradigm for Christian living was that God has a detailed plan of things for us to do during our lives. I believed that we could leave this world knowing that we had "fought the good fight" if we accomplished everything on that list. For some years now, I have understood that the doing of the Christian life is the result of His life flowing through us and not our own determination. However, only recently did it occur to me that we also glorify Him by *not* doing the things He doesn't lead us to do. For some of us, "doing" comes much easier than "not doing."

As I prayed when I read the prayer of Jesus, it proved to be one of the times when I immediately heard God speak through a thought He placed in my mind. "You need to recognize what it is that I have given you to do and focus on *that*," I heard Him say. The word that He put in my mind illuminated the busyness of my current lifestyle like a bright camera flash showing the clutter inside a dark closet.

In that moment, I realized it wasn't that He wanted me to be sure to accomplish the things on some Divine To Do list He had written for my lifetime. To the contrary and to my surprise, He wanted me to erase some of the things on the list I had unconsciously made in an attempt to accomplish as much as I could do. "Cease striving and know that I am God" (Psalm 46:8) is the most difficult command some of us will ever encounter.

I have understood that life is "in Him" and not "for Him," but in spite of knowing the truth, I still sometimes find myself with a propensity toward *doing* more than *being*. In moments of frustration I have said to Melanie, "I can teach truth about resting in Him. I just can't live it." The fact is that old habits die hard. Christian growth is a process in which we gradually advance, sometimes almost imperceptibly. As the old saying goes, "I'm not where I want to be, but thank God, I'm not where I used to be."

I long lived with the philosophy of an old man who once told me about the pills the doctor had prescribed that he take once a day: "If one will do me good, two will do me twice as much good." In his own convoluted logic, that kind of thinking seemed to make sense. I have used that type of ridiculous reasoning about my own lifestyle many times in life. In reality, taking more than the Great Physician has prescribed isn't better—it's toxic and will eventually create problems which ultimately destroy our spiritual health.

Less May Be More

It blasphemes one of the most sacred tenets of some evangelicals to suggest that perhaps they need to do less, not more. Grace is already susceptible enough to the recurring charges of passivity without people being told that they may need less activity in their lives. The "Just Do It" dogma is just as important to many contemporary Christians as is the deity of Christ.

The fact remains, however, that religious hyperactivity is a tick that slowly sucks the lifeblood out of our intimacy with God. God didn't invite you to be His maid, but His bride. Do we serve Him? Of course, but it always is to be the natural expression of our love for Him. Otherwise, it becomes a barrier to genuine intimacy.

Well-meaning Christians often find themselves in a place similar to the man adrift at sea in a life raft. Because he is dying of thirst, he begins to drink the seawater around him. The salt water causes him to become more thirsty, and his thirst causes him to drink even more sea-water. This vicious cycle will ultimately bring death.

Thus is the fate of the Christian who believes that doing more is the remedy for his thirst. Sometimes the answer to our deepest need is met when we understand that the best way to advance may be to retreat, remembering that God's ways are not our ways. Blaise Pascal said, "The sole cause of man's unhappiness is that he does not know how to stay quietly in his room." It isn't frenzy, but faith that facilitates intimacy.

Lost in the Woods of Busyness

One time I found myself lost in the woods alone. It was late at night, and a friend and I were going fishing. We had left our car parked on the side of a road and had gone through the woods down to the water's edge where our boat was tied. The plan was that we would load the boat with the supplies we had brought from the car; then he would take the boat across the lake to a bridge on the other side where I would drive the car, park it, and meet him.

I pushed the boat off, moving it away from the shoreline, and turned to go back through the woods to my car. However, as I began to make my way back, it didn't take long for me to become disoriented. The night shadows and muted colors caused every path to look the same. After walking for 30 minutes on a course that I knew would have only taken ten if it were the right one, I began to realize that I was probably lost.

I was a little nervous at first, but I told myself that I would eventually come upon the road and the car. An hour later, I knew I was in trouble when I found myself off the path and fighting my way through thick undergrowth filled with night sounds I didn't recognize. I had absolutely no idea which direction to head anymore. Instinctively I began to walk faster…and faster…and faster. After a while I realized that increasing my speed wasn't accomplishing anything except to make me tired.

I sat down to rest for a moment, telling myself that I needed to calm down and think this situation through more carefully. As I sat there, I glanced up toward the sky. Above me I saw my answer. It was a power line. I reasoned that the line had to lead *somewhere* and that I would simply follow it until it led me back to civilization.

That is exactly what I did, and my plan worked. After a long walk, the line led me back to a side road, which I then followed to the highway and to my car. It was a scary experience that to this day has kept me out of the woods alone at night.

My trek through the woods parallels the journey of many Christians' lives. Because we aren't sure how to get where we want to be, we simply walk faster and faster. In the process, we are accomplishing nothing but exhausting ourselves. In an effort to reach our goals, we become driven to increasing activity and effort, which only serves to exhaust us physically, emotionally, and spiritually. We seem stuck in a phase of spiritual growth that Kelly called "adolescent development" and "an awkward stage of religious busyness in the kingdom of God."[4]

What we need to do is stop running, sit down, and rest. Whenever we take that simple step, God will show us the "power line," which has been there all along. Only then can we follow it and find our way out of the woods and back to the main road of resting in Christ.

Gifts Gone Amuck

This compulsive drivenness of our culture certainly finds fertile soil within the modern church. Some of the fastest-growing churches in America are built around the premise that it is better to burn out for God than to rust out. Such a philosophy ignores the fact that either way, you're *out*. We have often been so obsessed with doing the activity of the Christian life, that we have lost Jesus in the shuffle of our busyness.

Even the most basic characteristics of a grace-filled life sometimes become routine, driven by discipline instead of desire. God allows us to experience His grace through spiritual gifts that He intends to be conduits through which He pours out His love into our lives. They don't create the intimacy, but provide an environment in which we can enjoy it. For example, consider these three: the

Bible, prayer, and the church. Each are meant to be set-tings—as inviting as a candlelight dinner—in which we experience His love. They are gifts to us from Him. They are ways in which we can sing the love songs of our hearts back and forth with Jesus.

The Bible *isn't* an instruction manual. It's a love letter with personalized notes to each of us that can only be really seen as the Holy Spirit shows them to us. Prayer is a supernatural and mystical action by which two lovers whisper to each other. Church life is a kingdom party where we come to the dance and celebrate this unbeliev-ably rich life He has given us—at no cost to us whatso-ever.

Legalistic religion denies all of that and turns His gifts into our obligations. It strips us of joyful intimacy and has the gall to turn God's grace gifts to us into religious duty. It causes you to feel like you would upon finding out that a neighbor has given your young child a puppy. Your neighbor may call it a gift, but you're the one who has to take care of it. Legalism may *call* the "spiritual disciplines" a gift, but that is as far as it goes. Now you are expected to maintain it, and nothing so quickly destroys inspiration as obligation.

Consider the three gifts I have mentioned, and note how *performance-based legalism* addresses each of them:

♦ **Bible study:** Who wouldn't acknowledge that the Bible is God's revelation to us? God speaks through His written Word. Is it unreasonable that He should expect that we must spend time every day in His Word? A daily devotional time in God's Word would seem to be a must for sincere Christians. Are you spending time reading the Bible every day of your life? How much time do you give to the Word of God? Do you hurriedly read a short pas-sage just so you can know you have done your duty for the day, or do you commit yourself to the discipline of ongoing Bible study? You must study your Bible if you really want to experience spiritual growth.

(Are you motivated to get into the Bible at this point?)

• **Prayer:** Few believers would argue that at the very least, we must be faithful in prayer. How often must one pray? The Bible says that we must "pray without ceasing." Would less than an hour a day qualify as constant prayer? Consider the needs of your family and friends. What about the needs of the world? How much time do you spend praying each day? Don't you think that we must pay the price in prayer if God is going to move in our circumstances?

(Are you inspired yet?)

• **Church life:** While many have forsaken the church, most Christians would agree that to be a good Christian, one must attend church faithfully. If a man comes home to his wife *most* of the time, but spends the night with somebody else now and then, is he considered faithful? Are you *faithful* in church participation? It is commonly recognized that we must come together with God's people since the Bible *does* say that we are not to forsake the assembling of ourselves together. Attending church isn't an option, it is a must.

(Ready to go yet?)

Legalism says we *must* read the Bible. We *must* pray. We *must* attend church. How do the previous three paragraphs affect you? (It is embarrassing for me to admit that they were easy to write because that's the way I preached for so many years.) Do you feel edified by those three paragraphs? Encouraged? Uplifted and motivated to do better? I doubt it. If so, legalism doesn't offend you at all—which should be a wake-up call. Remember that I asked you to consider these three areas as *legalism* would address them.

I intentionally used the word "must" ten times in those three paragraphs to illustrate the effect that a performance-based perspective on life in Christ produces. Legalism causes one to feel beaten down, judged, condemned (see 2 Corinthians 3:6-9). It takes the gifts which God has given us and turns them upside down, telling us that those very things are *our* gifts to God.

Enslaved by legalism, we read the Bible for Him. We pray because we think He is pleased by it. We attend church because He wants us to do it. We think we are doing God a favor when we do these things. In reality this is foolishness. It's Christianity turned inside out and made into an empty superstition, born of a belief that's completely out of sync with divine reality.

Aspects of Spirit-filled living, which flow naturally from the lifestyle of one walking in grace, become a millstone around the neck of one ensnared by legalism. I have used Bible study, prayer, and church life as examples because they tend to be primary targets of legalism. It takes what God intended to bring us real pleasure and turns it into nothing more than a religious performance.

You aren't doing God any favors by reading the Bible, praying, going to church, or doing anything else in an effort to please Him. It goes without saying that each is an integral part of authentic faith, but once these grace gifts have been submerged beneath the stagnant waters of dead religion, they lose all life. They no longer have legitimate meaning, neither to the believer nor to God.

Bible study no longer is a joy, it's a job. Prayer is no longer a romantic conversation. It becomes a "quiet time" which we must observe like the misbehaving child who is sent to his room for a "time out." Church attendance becomes nothing more than a weary responsibility or a social event.

Driven religious fervor becomes a one-night stand repeated over and over and over again. There may be a shallow gratification in one-night stands, but nobody would ever mistake such fleeting pleasure for genuine intimacy. God offers you much more than that. He wants you to experience Him and all of His gifts as a natural part of the soothing rhythms of grace. However, to know that kind of intimacy, we must stop our religious hyperventilating, calm down, and stop to smell the roses. God doesn't need you to break the three-minute-mile barrier for Him. He just wants you to enjoy Him, knowing that everything else in your life will flow out of that.

Jesus didn't come to make us religious superstars. Far from it—He came to deliver us *from* empty religion, even orthodox, time-honored religion. Jesus came to bring us into intimacy with God through Himself. In His earthly days, as in our day, those most offended by Him were the religionists who built their reputation by keeping their golden idols polished to a brighter shine than anybody else's in town.

The idols are their own particular rules of the road that must be observed as they speed down the highway they call "Christian living." Their display case is filled with the specific idols that most easily fit their own personality and temperament, and they judge everybody else by whether or not they live up to their own personal standards. People are incidental. What matters instead to the legalist is people's *behavior*.

Even Jesus wasn't a good churchman by the standards of the religionists of His day. He didn't live up to what they thought He ought to be. To them, He had no convictions. He appeared to compromise the purity and integrity of their values by doing things like healing people on the Sabbath, by eating with the crooks (publicans) and party-animals (sinners) of His day. He was a friend of the hookers and homeless. He didn't separate Himself far enough from the riffraff like every good churchman knew one should do. Consequently, He lost His testimony with the Pharisees, an incidental matter which didn't seem to bother Him at all. Jesus cared more about relationships than reputation. He still does.

A legitimate Christian lifestyle gently flows like water along a riverbank, refreshing all who happen to stumble upon its banks. It isn't a flash flood of activity that honors God. He doesn't lead us that way, but instead He has chosen to make "[us] lie down in green pastures. He leads [us] beside quiet waters [where] He restores [our] soul" (Psalm 23).

God loves you so much that He wants to deliver you from the misery of *must* into the triumph of *trust*. You have nothing to prove by a frantic pace. It isn't possible to hear the still, small voice whispering when you're running at breakneck speed. God invites you to stop and rest. Understand that the Bible, prayer, and church life are His gifts to you, not yours to Him.

It was a strange thing to me that I seemed to hear God speak to me while I was taking a shower more often than any other time. I commented on that fact to my wife one day. Melanie pointed out that it might be because that was the only time in my day when I consistently became relatively quiet and still.

I have decided that I'm not going to make God take a shower with me just to talk to me. My life has begun to change in many ways since I determined to rearrange my priorities, as reflected by my schedule. I want to move beyond the adolescent stage of religious busyness and begin to plumb the depths of my loving Father who has patiently nurtured me along.

Are you hungry to know Him more deeply? Then leave the religious rat race and let the only race you run be the one that takes you straight to Him. I'm discovering that even if we are spiritually retarded or have Spiritual Attention Deficit Disorder, there is a Great Physician who can cure any problem. All we need to do is trust Him, and He will do the rest.

Dear Father,
So many things in my life compete with You for my attention. Enable me to prioritize the responsibilities in my life so that intimacy with You isn't choked out by less-important things. Cause me to live righteously, not just religiously. May all that I do be motivated by nothing less than love for You.

G.R.A.C.E. GROUP QUESTIONS

1. This chapter lightheartedly mentions potential spiritual disabilities such as "spiritual retardation" and "Spiritual Attention Deficit Disorder." What other "spiritual disabilities" can you identify in the modern church? Which ones do you experience?

2. What are some impediments to intimacy with Christ that threaten the modern church? How can Christian ministries help people overcome these impediments and develop real intimacy with God?

3. "Panting feverishness" was mentioned as a possible slogan for some churches. What are other possible slogans which reflect the type of ministry present in churches you have attended?

4. Read John 17:4. What will be necessary for you to be able to say these words when you come to the end of your earth-life?

5. This chapter describes the way that performance-based legalism would address the matters of Bible reading, prayer and church participation. How are these areas to be viewed from a grace orientation?

6. One paragraph in this chapter begins with this sentence: "Even Jesus wasn't a good churchman by the standards of the religionists of His day." How would He be viewed in the typical church of today *if He disguised Himself so that the people didn't know who He was?* What positive qualities would your church appreciate about Jesus if He were a member there? What would they find hard to accept about Him?

8

The Fire Burned

ON THE DAY OF PENTECOST WHEN GOD'S SPIRIT came upon His people, He presented Himself to them as tongues of fire, resting on each one (see Acts 2:1-3). *Fire*—the word itself is charged with imagery of unbearable intensity and unquenchable force. The writer of Hebrews plainly says, "For our God is a consuming fire" (Hebrews 12:29).

When Moses was on the mountaintop alone with God, the only thing the people down below could see when they looked toward the top of the mountain was a consuming fire (see Exodus 24:17). Later, when he described God to the people, he said, "For the LORD your God is a consuming fire, a jealous God" (Deuteronomy 4:24).

God's desire for you is that you would be *consumed* by Him. His love rages for you as a passionate inferno which refuses to be quenched until He has subdued every part of your being. He is jealous for you and will not rest until you are so engulfed in the flames of His love that everything else in life is incidental by comparison.

It isn't without reason that a sexually charged person is called *hot*. Even an animal is considered to be "in heat" at the time when the urge to mate is greatest. The word carries the idea of being possessed by desire that cannot be hidden and that can only be restrained with great effort.

At the risk of sounding irreverent, it must be pointed out that God is *hot* for you. Don't be offended by such an application. It isn't about sexuality, but it *is* about the essence of sexuality—union. God wants you to find complete pleasure and total fulfillment by understanding and experiencing the union you share with Him (see 1 Corinthians 6:16-17). His purpose is that you should live in union with Him in the fire of His passion *for you*.

After the fire of God consumed his life, Thomas Kelly was repeatedly heard to say, "It is wonderful. I have been literally melted down by the love of God."[1] Others who have attested to intense moments of awareness of God's presence have done so using terms associated with heat, sometimes metaphorically and occasionally literally.

Catherine of Siena prayed, "O fire surpassing every fire because You alone are the fire that burns without consuming!...Yet your consuming does not distress the soul but fattens her with insatiable love." The French mystic Madame Guyon wrote, "I slept not all night, because Thy love, O my God, flowed in me like delicious oil, and burned as a fire..."[2] On the night of his conversion to Christ in 1654, Blaise Pascal wrote: "Fire. The God of Abraham, the God of Isaac, the God of Jacob...Certainty, certainty, emotion, joy, peace, God of Jesus Christ."[3] Transformed by the intimate love of Jesus Christ, St. John of the Cross wrote a book entitled, *Living Flame of Love*.

Knowing God's Love at Every Level

The point isn't that you should experience the same thing that others have experienced. God's expression of love for His bride is universal, yet at the same time it is deeply personal and unique to each of us. The key is in understanding that God has a burning love not only for Christians in general, but also for *you* specifically.

It isn't enough to simply acknowledge intellectually that God loves you. To restrict God's love to the intellect alone will greatly limit our ability to enjoy Him. The raging fire of His love seeks to permeate your mind, your emotions, and your will. Then, having ravaged *your* soul, His love will leap from your life, through your actions, onto those around you, like a forest fire that jumps from one tree to another.

God wants you to both know and feel His love. There seems to be a tendency in many circles to either focus on experiencing God through the mind to the exclusion of the emotions, or vice versa. One group accuses the other of emotionalism, while the second views the former as being either afraid or ignorant of the Holy Spirit. One may claim to be led by the Bible, while the other professes to be led by the Spirit, but neither extreme is a biblical position.

God wants His love to invade every part of our being. A balanced life is one in which we clearly understand His love intellectually, deeply experience His love emotionally, and purposefully live out of His love volitionally. With life in balance, the written Word guides us objectively and the living Word within guides us subjectively.

From out of the center of His love, we are then able to live the carefree, abundant life that Jesus Christ came to give us. God wants you to *enjoy* life. He wants you to gulp it down by the gallon! Isn't that the real desire of every Christian?

Here's how author Jeff Imbach expresses it:

> We have a powerful innate drive to drink deeply of life and of God—to come to the end of our lives saying that we've truly lived. That this urge belongs

at the heart of a person's spiritual life makes the circle complete. Life is good!

There is, however, another side. While we long to live this way, most of us are actually terrified to do so. Confronted with the opportunity to dance with life, we cling to our inhibitions and fears and our little ways of skulking in the shadows of uninvolvement. We may tap our toes, but we're firmly glued to our chairs. We aren't easily persuaded to get up and dance.[4]

Get Up and Dance

I have long felt the urge to dance with life. I'm not sure if it is a sad commentary on the state of modern Christendom or of spiritual deficits in my own life, but the first time I found the desires for an authentic life articulated in the way that most closely fit my own was from a source outside the church. In fact, it was from one outside the faith.

As I read Henry David Thoreau's *Walden,* the irony of the fact that he wasn't a Christian didn't stop me from hearing the clarion call from within my own heart to experience the deepest and fullest that life has to offer. His desire to "suck the marrow from life" described my own zest for living. What Thoreau thought he could find in nature, I knew could be found in Jesus Christ.

Imagine a life in which the fire of God so consumes you that you lose all inhibitions, a life in which you charge forth confidently into every day with the assurance that God is guiding every step you take. This life isn't imaginary, it's real! We experience it when we live from the blazing glory of His love for us.

Tony Campolo once said, "Most of us are tiptoeing through life so we can reach death safely. We should be praying, 'If I should wake before I die.' Life can get away from you. Don't be satisfied with just pumping blood." There is an abundant life for the taking for those who have the assurance of God's unconditional love and commitment to those on whom He has set His passion.

When consumed with the fire of God's love, you can say with the Psalmist, "Our God is forever and ever; He will guide us until death" (Psalm 48:14). With the confidence of David when he was surrounded and outnumbered in battle by the Philistines, we can shout to the world with assurance, "This I *know*, that God is for me!" (Psalm 56:9).

What is the key to living out of this fire, this Divine force which empowers us to rise above the mass mediocrity of the modern church? How can we reclaim our God-given experience of the supernatural life which is our birthright? How can we be in this turbulent and transient world and still live in a way which demonstrates that we are firmly anchored in the Eternal?

The answer, of course, is Christ. The answer is *always* Christ. Knowing who we are in Him and who He is in us is the cornerstone upon which everything else in life is set. I have written other books which specifically focus on the believer's identity in Christ.[5] Consequently, I won't be redundant on the foundational aspects of our identity at this point. However, it is necessary to clearly state that what follows in this and the next chapter has the potential for greatest results only if these truths are grounded in your identity in Him.

Knowing our union with God through Christ is of paramount importance to the abundant life. However, one question I am continually asked is, "*How* do we consistently abide in Christ, allowing Him to live His life through us?" The question is loaded in one sense because it easily lends itself to an answer which delineates particular steps one may take to abide in Christ. We must tread carefully when we approach the word *how* in the Christian walk lest we drift from the *Who*, namely Jesus Christ—the Source and Center of an authentic Christian lifestyle. *How* isn't unapproachable under grace, but should be attended to with caution.

We are getting dangerously close to legalism when we begin to list steps for a life of faith. While it is true that the Apostle Paul clearly laid down "the how" of day-to-day living, he did so only after clearly establishing the foundational truths of identity. For instance, his letters to the church at Corinth are filled with instruction about how to live, but the very first words he wrote pointed to the identity they already knew (see 1 Corinthians 1:2-9). Only on that foundation were the practical applications for life made.

Even when the steps aren't intended to be taken in a legalistic way, people interpret information through their own unique paradigm. If their grid is one of legalism, great momentum works against a clear understanding. We know we are being pulled away from grace by the undertow of legalism when we become more engulfed in "ought to" than "want to." Law scolds people into submission, but offers no strength by which they can respond. Grace always encourages *and* energizes us to live the life to which God has called us.

Abiding in Christ isn't achieved by successfully following certain steps. It's an act of faith by which we simply choose to believe that He is our life, that He will express Himself through us, and then act as if He is doing that very thing at this very moment. Abundant living isn't found in a plan, but is found in the *Person* of Jesus Christ. That fact can't be overstated or emphasized too many times.

God's Grace in Solitude and Meditation

Having made that point, there is one element in the grace walk that I have found to be an amazing conduit through which I often experience His indwelling life and love. It is an act of grace which strengthens my sense of union with Him in a wonderful way. I'm talking about the biblical practice of solitude and meditation. The matter of solitude will be considered in this chapter and the practice of meditation in the next. I have found these two to be grace gifts from God which have strengthened me immeasurably in my pursuit of intimacy with Him.

Solitude is often avoided at all costs in contemporary culture, despite its biblical and historical precedent as an integral part of communion with God. Contemporary society has been inundated by a torrent of *words*. Hearing God speak in our crowded lifestyles is like hoping to hear a person across a crowded room speak over the unintelligible chatter that surrounds us.

Henri Nouwen describes our "wordy world" this way:

> Wherever we go we are surrounded by words: words softly whispered, loudly proclaimed, or angrily screamed; words spoken, recited, or sung; words on records, in books, on walls, or in the sky; words in many sounds, many colors, or many forms; words to be heard, read, seen, or glanced at; words which flicker off and on, move slowly, dance, jump, or wiggle. Words, words, words! They form the floor, the walls, and the ceiling of our existence.[6]

To enjoy quiet intimacy with God, we must withdraw *by intention* from our crowded, wordy world. The Bible records occasions when Jesus Himself withdrew into a solitary place (see Mark 1:35; Luke 4:42). If Jesus thought it necessary to withdraw from the demands on His time and ministry to commune with God in quietness, how much more important must it be to us?

An incident in the gospel of Mark brings into focus the importance of solitude. The disciples had just returned from a successful ministry trip where they had seen tremendous results through preaching, casting out devils, and healing. No doubt with great enthusiasm "the apostles gathered together with Jesus, and reported to Him all that they had done and taught" (Mark 6:30).

What would you think the response of Jesus would be at a moment like that? If He had learned how to respond from the preaching I did for many years, He might have said, "Good job! Don't quit now! Our momentum is going, and let's keep it that way! Boys, get out there and preach the kingdom!"

That's the kind of leadership I gave for a long time. After all, I reasoned, the devil never takes time out, so why should we? However, the response of Jesus is different from the kind of response I would have given.

> He said to them, "Come away by yourselves to a secluded place and rest a while." For there were many people coming and going, and they did not even have time to eat. They went away in the boat to a secluded place by themselves (Mark 6:31-32).

At a time when the disciples reported on how well things were going, Jesus said, "Great! Now, rest awhile." That kind of advice hasn't typically fit my personality type or the way I've been wired to live my Christian life. Even now, it doesn't come easily to me. Something inside me feels like I'm wasting time when I rest, unless it's at night when I'm in bed—and even then I sometimes find my mind racing like a Pentium computer.

Jesus said to His disciples, "Rest." Do you hear that word resonating somewhere deep inside you? For many, it's easier to be busy with activity than to patiently wait on the Lord in solitude. It's a lesson some of us must learn and relearn all our lives. It's a lesson I am just beginning to learn.

After being clearly shown by the Holy Spirit that I needed to realign my schedule to allow time for solitude, I had responsibilities to attend to in our office in Mexico.[7] It was during that time that the deadline for this book was quickly approaching. I determined that in order to escape potential distractions and to be able to work on the manuscript with no interruptions, I would spend an extra week in Ajijic, a small town on Lake Chapala, about an hour from Guadalajara. I emailed close friends and asked them to pray for me while I was there that the Lord would enable me to accomplish much.

God surely has a sense of humor. For several days, the time I spent writing flowed in such a way that made it clear God was blessing my work. Then one morning I awoke early and turned on the laptop. When lunchtime came, I was still sitting there staring at a blank screen. I felt brain-dead. "Uh, Lord...what's going on?" I asked. "You know, I have a deadline coming soon. This sure would be a good time for You to enable me to write."

Once again, just as He had done in that small cabin in Southern Georgia, God refused to endorse my deadline. My writing stalled, just as before.

I decided to eat lunch and walk around the quaint community's cobblestone streets and picturesque environment to clear my mind. A couple of hours later I went back to my room and sat down. Nothing. Didn't God know that I was on a mission? Hadn't I set this time aside to do the work *He* had led me to do? For the rest of the day—zero. Not a word.

At nine o'clock that night, I called Melanie, who was back at home in the states, and I whined like a spoiled child about my day. "I don't know what's going on," I said, "but if something doesn't happen tomorrow, I'm coming home." I hung up the telephone and sat down, opening my Bible. "Lord," I prayed as I opened it, "please speak to me. What am I doing? What am I *not* doing? You know I've tried to get this work done today. *What do you want me to do?*"

I feel a little self-conscious describing what happened then because it's not something I recommend as a way to hear from God. It's a childish approach to the Bible that will cause serious students of Scripture to cringe (maybe the Lord spoke through this method because I was *acting* like a child). I opened my Bible and it *fell open* to Psalms, which I had been reading from for months. As I looked down at the opened page, my eyes fell on Psalm 4:4, where the following words seem to jump off the page in response to my question, "What do you want me to do?"

The verse says, "Meditate in your heart upon your bed and *be still*"! (emphasis added). I couldn't help but snicker out loud, all alone. Here I was trying—no, *struggling* to write about *resting* in Christ in solitude, yet even alone in a foreign country I found myself predisposed to live on the fast track. God wouldn't jump through my hoops, and when He did speak, all He said was, "You go to bed and think about this."

The purpose for this self-disclosure is to assure you that the lessons about solitude and meditation aren't fully mastered by many, if any. We are all in process. Perhaps we all will spend our lifetime learning the lesson little by little.

The Sound of Silence

Noise may be our worst enemy. Our environment seems to demand our attention, distracting us from that which really matters. Thomas à Kempis said at the beginning of the fifteenth century, "For that is the cause why there are so few contemplative persons to be found, for that few can wholly withdraw themselves from things created and perishing." He thought they had it bad! Over a half a millennium later, things have only become worse.

Gordon MacDonald describes our dilemma well:

> Few of us can fully appreciate the terrible conspiracy of noise there is about us, noise that denies us the silence and solitude we need for this cultivation of the inner garden. It would not be hard to believe that the archenemy of God has conspired to surround us at every conceivable point in our lives with the interfering noises of civilization that, when left unmuffled, usually drown out the voice of God. He who walks with God will tell you plainly, God does not ordinarily shout to make Himself heard. As Elijah discovered, God tends to whisper in the garden.[8]

The fire of God's love for you cannot be extinguished, but perhaps nothing so quickly douses out the flame of our *awareness* as noise. Jeremiah said, "The LORD is good to those who wait for Him, To the person who seeks Him. It is good that he waits *silently* for the salvation of the LORD" (Lamentations 3:25-26, emphasis added). Intimacy with God and continuous noise are mutually exclusive. If there are to be times of conscious intimacy with Him, there *must* be times of silence and solitude. God will not shout over the clamor of our cluttered lives.

Do you really want to explore the depths of intimacy with God? Do you hear an inner voice calling you to a simpler, quieter place? The Divine Lover is calling you to your own secret place, shared by you two alone. Thomas Kelly writes:

> You may see it over the margin and wistfully long to slip into that amazing Center where the soul is at home with God. Be very faithful to that wistful longing. It is the Eternal Goodness calling you to return Home, to feed upon green pastures and walk beside still waters and live in the peace of the

Shepherd's presence. It is the life *beyond* fevered strain.[9]

There is an awakening among many believers today who are no longer satisfied with the hustle and bustle generally known as the Christian life. Call it the deeper life, the contemplative life, or whatever you will. By any name, this quality of Christian life is conceived in divine intimacy and born in quiet moments spent between two lovers. Many Christians who are dissatisfied with the emptiness of the noise are hearing His gentle call to something deeper, richer.

One day, my friend Barry gave me a copy of *Christianity Today* which contained an article about Leighton Ford and his "new ministry." Ford is the brother-in-law of Billy Graham and worked with the Billy Graham Evangelistic Association for 30 years. The magazine article described him as being "known for his revival evangelism, sweaty preaching, and making thousands of new coverts in a single night."[10] His ministry was the type that almost every preacher I knew wanted to have, but the article went on to say that, "After a globetrotting lifetime of service to wherever God—and brother-in-law Billy Graham—called him, the 70-year-old Ford now spends most of his time listening to God's still, small voice."

Listening to God's still, small voice? Leighton Ford's ministry was well known. I knew he had been very successful, according to most people's standards. Now, after all of his preaching, with so many conversions, and after such global impact, he decided to give himself to a contemplative lifestyle focused on mentoring and being mentored? It must have been a gentle, sweet Voice to lure a man away from his previous lifestyle.

Reading about his life choice only reinforced what I knew God was telling me about slowing down my own pace to allow time for solitude and meditation. I had already revised my calendar for the following year, canceling some of the things I had previously scheduled. Now, reading about his discovery of a new way only fanned the flame of my desire to know more.

The words of Thomas Kelly further intensified my desire. He wrote:

> I wish I might emphasize how a life becomes simplified when dominated by faithfulness to a few concerns. Too many of us have had too many irons in the fire. We get distracted by the intellectual claim to our interest in a thousand and one good things, and before we know it we are pulled and hauled breathlessly along by an over-burdened program of good committees and good undertakings. I am persuaded that this fevered life of church workers is not wholesome. Undertakings get plastered on from the outside because we can't turn down a friend. Acceptance of service on a weighty committee should really depend upon an answering imperative within us, not merely upon rational calculation of the factors involved. The concern-oriented life is ordered and organized from within. And we learn to say *No* as well as *Yes* by attending to the guidance of inner responsibility.[11]

The Fire Burns in Stillness

Stillness. It was into the stillness of an empty void that God spoke and said, "Let there be," and all that is came into existence. It was in the stillness of a barren desert that a man met God at a burning bush and was commissioned to lead His people to freedom. It was in the stillness of the night that a baby's cry could be heard in Bethlehem, announcing salvation to the world. It was another still night when that same child would cry to His Father in a garden, "Not my will, but Thine be done." It was in the stillness of an early morning that a stone was rolled away and an occupied tomb would forever be emptied. Stillness—God's showcase.

The fire of God's love burns brightly in the stillness. It's in that stillness that the distractions and cares of the world fade away in the same way that outside noises are muted when we make love to our beloved. It's in that stillness that we're able to give our thoughts, our feelings, and our will completely to Him in uninhibited abandon.

It's in that stillness that we are able to meditate—to *muse* on the Person and the loving words of the One whose passion burns for us—until we are irreparably and eternally ignited by the Flame. It's in that stillness that we gasp with delight along with the Psalmist, "My heart was hot within me; while I was musing, *the fire burned*" (Psalm 39:3, emphasis added).

Dear Father,

My desire is for You to free me from the noise that drowns out Your voice and the music of Your love. I want to experience quiet, intimate moments with You. Teach me to "come apart and rest" as You instructed Your disciples. Show me how to structure my responsibilities so that Your fire can consistently burn within my heart.

G.R.A.C.E. GROUP QUESTIONS

1. Read the account of the day of Pentecost in Acts 2. List four characteristics of God which could be compared to fire.

2. What does it mean to you to "get up and dance with life?" What are some common reasons why people are reluctant to live in carefree abandon? What does a person's life look like who has abandoned himself completely into the life of God?

3. Read Mark 1:35; Luke 4:42. What do you believe were Jesus' reasons for withdrawing to a solitary place? What benefits can Christians today expect to experience by embracing times of solitude in their lives? Are you comfortable with solitude in your own life? Why or why not?

4. Read the quote in this chapter from Gordon MacDonald about the "conspiracy of noise" in our culture. What are the noises that are most likely to interfere with your times

of solitude with Christ? Read Lamentations 3:25-26 and explain what God is saying to you from that passage.

5. List three things not mentioned in this chapter that God did in an environment of stillness. What is the most significant thing you have experienced from God in times of stillness in your own life?

6. Set aside two days during the next month to do nothing but spend contemplative time with God. Ask Him to speak to you, revealing His heart to you.

9

The Holy Hideaway

THE FRUSTRATIONS OF DAILY ROUTINE FADE like shadows disappearing under the brilliance of a midday sun. Demanding urgencies are made to lie down and be quiet like a whining child who finally goes to bed. Issues which ordinarily insist on a place of high priority are rearranged so that, at the moment, they become trivial. There are still matters which will need to be handled, and they will be—in time. But for now, you are invited to a secret garden which transcends time. Life outside this place will once again clamor for attention. However, for now, none of those things matter in the presence of the Divine Lover. Time seems to stand still before His timeless beauty.

This garden is a place to which *you* are invited; to which you are *enticed* by the Holy Spirit. It is a place of prayerful meditation. It is a secret rendezvous in a *sacred* place shared by two lovers whose greatest joy is to be alone together, reveling in each other's love. It is your own holy hideaway where you and Jesus have the opportunity to celebrate your union together in the privacy of a sacred center where nothing and nobody can disrupt your intimacy.

It is in those private moments together that we find ourselves so secure in His acceptance, so aware of His love, that the issues of our innermost being begin to surface in prayer. We empty our hearts in the presence of the One who will never reject us for any reason. Like lovers who lie awake talking through the night, we find ourselves sharing our darkest secrets and our deepest hurts. We talk about the dreams that we cannot let go and the disappointments that will not let us go.

In complete awareness of His genuine interest in us, it isn't necessary to fluff up our language with religious jargon. In the presence of His tender acceptance, there is no need to try to suppress the issues of our lives which are uncomfortable to discuss. In this holy hideaway, we have the deep abiding sense that we are home at last. We know that this is a safe place, where love prevails. It is a place where we *want* to be absolutely vulnerable and transparent.

What is this sacred place where we may meet Jesus Christ? It is a place of prayer, but it's more than that. It is a place of *meditation*. For many years I found consistency in prayer to be a challenge. It was a *discipline*, something to do because the Bible says to do it. I felt guilty about not particularly wanting to pray much of the time. I *wanted* to want to pray, but when I prayed it was often an intellectual exercise aimed at producing a positive spiritual outcome. It was classic legalistic prayer—put something into it just to get something out of it. Make spiritual progress based on what I do, like a person does sit-ups because he knows it is good for him even if he doesn't particularly enjoy it.

Sometimes I would try to get "psyched up" to feel God's presence. There certainly were genuine moments of

His awareness, but I still generally felt that in some unexplainable way my prayer life was deficient. There was a shallowness to my prayers that left me wanting more.

Since beginning to understand prayer within the context of meditation, things have changed. I have come to understand that Jesus has never called us to a religious "quiet time," but has invited us to join Him in a private rendezvous where He can lavish His love on us.

We identify with the young bride who said,

> Like an apple tree among the trees of the forest,
>   so is my beloved among the young men.
> In his shade I took great delight and sat down,
>   And his fruit was sweet to my taste.
> He has brought me to his banquet hall,
>   And his banner over me is love
> (Song of Solomon 2:3-4).

Perhaps you have begun to experience Jesus Christ revealing Himself to you in more intimate ways. Maybe you hear His loving voice calling you to come, sit down, and let Him spread His love over you in moments of supernatural intimacy known through prayerful meditation.

You aren't being called to fulfill a religious discipline. Instead, you're invited to a time of loving interaction when Jesus Christ pours out His affection upon you. Once you become aware of His loving embrace, you can't get enough. From that moment on, you aren't simply seeking to have questions answered or needs met. From that moment forward, you will find yourself seeking *Him*.

Meditation Misunderstood

The whole concept of meditation is shrouded in mystery to many Christians. For some reason, the word evokes a negative connotation to many believers. Someone rightly said that "we tend to be down on the things we're not up

on." Many Christians aren't "up on" the subject of meditation. Writer Buck Anderson accurately describes the perception many of us have held:

> The word probably brings to mind a dimly lit,
> incense-filled room. On the floor sit several dedi-
> cated disciples in what must be very uncomfortable
> positions. Together, hoping to become "one" with
> their god, they incessantly chant their secret mantra,
> "Ommm, Ommm, Ommm."[1]

That certainly was my perception. Meditation seemed
like something done by people involved in *strange* reli-
gions, folks not playing with a full spiritual deck. I grew
up to be a good Protestant Christian and was leery of anything outside my own frame of reference. I heard the
word "meditation" thrown around at times, but generally
it was connected to *reading* the Bible, not meditating in
the true sense of the word. The only people I knew of
who practiced real meditation had bald heads, ate tofu,
and wore strange robes, none of which appealed to me.
Anderson continues:

> No Christian wants anything to do with the scene
> just described. We know the one true God is
> reached only through the "one mediator between
> God and men, the man Christ Jesus" (1 Timothy 2:5
> NIV). We recognize that any attempt to reach God
> outside of Christ is pagan.

> In recognizing this fact, however, I wonder if we
> have tossed the proverbial baby out with the bath
> water. I wonder [if], by our *correctly* rejecting med-
> itation as described above, we have incorrectly
> believed that any form of meditation is wrong and
> not for Christians.[2]

A Biblical Precedent

The Bible teaches the place of meditation in the lives of those who love God. Consider the following passages and what they have to say about meditation:

> ◆ Psalm 27:4 One thing I have asked from the LORD, that I shall seek: That I may dwell in the house of the LORD all the days of my life, To behold the beauty of the LORD And to meditate in His temple.

The presence of the physical tabernacle where God met His people was an Old Testament type which fore-shadowed a future *inner* tabernacle in which God would live inside His people under a new covenant. There is an inner place where God lives and longs for us to enjoy Him. The Lord is in His holy temple. The Apostle Paul described this temple saying, "Do you not know that *you* are a temple of God and that the Spirit of God dwells in you?" (1 Corinthians 3:16, emphasis added). God lives within you and desires that you not look to outside sources to fulfill you, but to look to Christ who resides within you.

> ◆ Psalm 63:6 When I remember You on my bed, I meditate on You in the night watches, For You have been my help.

> ◆ Psalm 77:6,12 I will remember my song in the night; I will meditate with my heart, And my spirit ponders...I will meditate on all Your work and muse on Your deeds.

> ◆ Psalm 119:15 I will meditate on Your precepts and regard Your ways. (See also Psalm 119:27, 48,78,148.)

- Psalm 143:5 I remember the days of old; I meditate on all Your doings; I muse on the work of Your hands.

A definition of meditation drawn from the Psalms could be this: "The act of focusing our undivided attention on God's indwelling presence, His works, His ways, and His words." It involves the emptying out of everything else that would interfere with our ability to be completely focused on Him. Biblical meditation exists when our whole being is intently riveted on Him.

Meditation as a form of prayer is simply emptying our busy minds of everything else so that we can be filled with nothing but Him. Eastern religious forms of meditation are wrong because they neither start nor finish with Jesus Christ. They simply stress emptying the mind. That's their goal—to be empty. Biblical meditation, on the other hand, is the act of emptying our minds so that we can be *filled* with the awareness of Christ Jesus.

This practice isn't a one-sided monologue in which we present our shopping list to God of all the things we want Him to give to us and do for us. (It's amazing how often Christians seem to get God confused with Santa Claus.) Instead, it's a *dialogue* in which we interact with Him, sometimes with words, at other times without words. It's a place where we leave the cares of the world outside the door and enter into a private room with God, and *He* sets the pace for what happens between us. We simply respond.

There is a passage in the New Testament that, although it doesn't specifically mention meditation, seems to point to its substance. In John 4, Jesus is talking to the Samaritan woman about her own spiritual needs. As unbelievers often do, she attempted to shift the focus off herself and her spiritual condition by trying to provoke a discussion about where a person should worship.

> "Our fathers worshiped in this mountain, and you people say that in Jerusalem is the place where men ought to worship." Jesus said to her, "Woman, believe Me, an hour is coming when neither in this mountain nor in Jerusalem will you worship the Father. You worship what you do not know; we worship what we know, for salvation is from the Jews. But an hour is coming, and now is, when the true worshipers will worship the Father in spirit and truth; for such people the Father seeks to be His worshipers. God is spirit, and those who worship Him must worship in spirit and truth" (John 4:20-24).

Jesus said that genuine worship isn't tied to a physical location, but is spiritual in essence. He said that God is *seeking* for people who move beyond the veneer of empty religious ritual, and into the place where worship is grounded in spiritual reality and ultimate truth. Is this the way you would describe worship in your own life?

Meditation, prayer, worship—while distinctions certainly can be made between the three, there is a sense in which they are all ingredients in the same recipe for intimacy with God. Animated by the Holy Spirit, each will reach out to encompass the others, integrating them into our lives so that we experience God, not casually, but in a deep way that brings transformation to our lives.

How does one learn the kind of worship that Jesus described? A worship which flows from our spirit and is guided by truth? The Lord, Himself, must teach us. Jean-Nicholas Grou wrote:

> Since prayer is a supernatural act, we must earnestly ask God to produce it in us, and then we must perform it tranquilly under His guidance. We must draw down divine grace by our favor and then we must cooperate with it without interfering with its

> effects. If God does not teach us, we shall never
> know thoroughly the nature of prayer.[3]

Do you *want* to experience the reality of Jesus Christ in prayer? As you read these pages, do you sense a swelling desire within you to experience greater intimacy with Him? Then be encouraged! That desire is the stirring of the Holy Spirit within you. It wouldn't be there otherwise, and the fact that He is stirring your desire isn't an indication of what He wants *you* to do. It is an indication of what *He* is going to do in you. Yield yourself to Him with a simple acknowledgment of faith, saying, "Yes, Lord! My desire is the same one expressed by your disciples—teach me to pray!"

Thomas Kelly writes:

> There *is* a last rock for your soul, a resting place of
> absolute peace and joy and power and radiance
> and security. There is a Divine Center into which
> your life can slip, a new and absolute orientation
> in God, a Center where you live with Him and out
> of which you see all of life, through new and
> radiant vision, tinged with new sorrows and pangs,
> new joys unspeakable and full of glory.[4]

An Invitation to Intimacy

There is nothing you can *do* to develop the grace of prayerful meditation. Like every other aspect of our lives, prayer is a work of God. To believe that by our own self-determination we can create a sense of intimacy with Him is to embrace a legalistic approach to spiritual growth. Legalistic efforts *never* give life, but *always* produce nothing but death and condemnation (see 2 Corinthians 3:7,9). Many Christians have sought to establish a strong prayer life, giving it their best effort with complete sincerity, only to ultimately come to the familiar place of inconsistency and discouragement.

Perhaps, however, you are sensing the invitation of the Divine Lover to join Him in a private place to which He wants to lead you. Maybe you can hear His voice saying about you, "I will allure her, bring her into the wilderness And speak kindly to her" (Hosea 2:14). If you sense a desire for this type of intimacy, be assured your desire is an invitation from Jesus Christ delivered to you by the Holy Spirit. Do you *want* to accept His invitation? He is whispering to you, "Come with me. There is *so much* I want to tell you!"

> Each of us can live such a life of amazing power and peace and serenity, of integration and confidence and simplified multiplicity, on one condition—that is, *if we really want to*. There is a divine Abyss within us all, a holy Infinite Center, a Heart, a Life who speaks in us and through us to the world. We have all heard this holy whisper at times. At times we have followed the Whisper, and amazing equilibrium of life, amazing effectiveness of living set in. But too many of us have heeded the Voice only at times...We have not surrendered *all else* to attend to it alone.[5]

Redefining the Meaning of Prayer

For many years, my prayer life was an activity that occurred primarily in my intellect. Prayer consisted of words formed in my mind and presented to God either vocally or mentally. Words are a fruit of our minds. Jean-Nicholas Grou noted that, "We need words to make ourselves intelligible to other people but not to the Spirit."[6] The Apostle Paul said the same when he noted that "the Spirit Himself intercedes for us with groanings too deep for words" (Romans 8:26).

Jesus said that true worship exists "in *spirit* and in truth." We pray from our spirit when we speak to God with what Grou calls "the voice of the heart." He says,

> You ask me what this voice of the heart is. It is love which is the voice of the heart. Love God and you will always be speaking to Him. The seed of love is growth in prayer. If you do not understand that, you have never yet either loved or prayed. Ask God to open your heart and kindle in it a spark of His love, and then you will begin to understand what praying really means.
>
> If it is the heart that prays, it is evident that sometimes, and even continuously, it can pray by itself without any help from words, spoken or conceived. Here is something which few people understand and which some even entirely deny. They insist that there must be definite and formal acts. They are mistaken, and God has not yet taught them how the heart prays.[7]

Not only are words unnecessary in prayer at times, but they may actually interfere with intimate communion with Jesus Christ. Even in the most intimate moments between a husband and wife, words are sometimes not spoken. They simply aren't necessary at the moment. As you share intimate moments with Jesus, you may discover several ways words may get in the way of intimacy.

♦ *Sometimes we hide behind words.*

Words sometimes actually may be a way we try to protect ourselves from complete honesty. A person who is stopped by the police for driving under the influence will often "give himself away" by his incessant talking. It's obvious that he's trying to hide something.

Sometimes we unconsciously do the same with God. We may seek to conceal our true selves by hiding behind many words. In the midst of silence, God may show you some things about yourself that have been hidden. Things which He wants to surface in order to deal with them, thus bringing you greater spiritual health and overall well-being.

♦ *Sometimes words restrict our prayer.*

Another fallacy in believing that prayer requires words is that it restricts prayer to the mind and mouth. Apart from words, God's Spirit may touch deep places in our emotions or may give new direction and resolve to our will. Our mind may not know our deepest needs, but the Holy Spirit knows. "A plan in the heart of a man is like deep water, But a man of understanding draws it out" (Proverbs 20:5). God has infinite capacity to draw up from the depth of our hearts the issues which need His healing touch. As His love washes over us during meditation, "deep calls to deep" (Psalm 42:7), and we find ourselves being miraculously refreshed in dry places that we didn't even know were there.

The benefit of healing that comes through prayerful meditation as we simply bask in the love of God can't be overstated. The frustrations and pains of our routine lifestyle quietly bow in humble submission before the Eternal Now and we see them for what they are—transitory, a puff of smoke, here today and gone tomorrow. Everything falls into its proper perspective in the presence of Eternal Life. Things that seem so important when we clutch them in the tight grip of our self-sufficient hands are revealed for what they are when we open our hands to Him in submission and adoration.

♦ *Sometimes words give us a false sense of spirituality.*

A final reason why we may need to redefine the meaning of prayer is that when we believe we have prayed because we have *said* the necessary words for the appropriate amount of time, we might gain a false sense of well-being. Just because one may "say prayers" doesn't mean he prayed. Jesus described two men who went to the temple to pray one day:

> Two men went up into the temple to pray, one a Pharisee and the other a tax collector. The Pharisee stood and was praying this to himself: "God, I thank You that I am not like the other people: swindlers, unjust, adulterers, or even like this tax collector. I fast twice a week; I pay tithes of all that I get."

> But the tax collector, standing some distance away, was even unwilling to lift up his eyes to heaven, but was beating his breast, saying, "God, be merciful to me, the sinner!"

> I tell you, this man went to his house justified rather than the other; for everyone who exalts himself will be humbled, but he who humbles himself will be exalted (Luke 18:10-14).

Legitimate prayer isn't defined by words, but by what is happening in the heart. A rote, routine, religious, rigor mortis-affected "quiet time" that is dutifully done right between brushing your teeth and heading out the door for work may be an insult to God. It's not the time given or words spoken that matter; it's the heart. The best prayer is to bow our heads and simply wait in quiet humility for God's Spirit to guide us in what to say or not say. Repentance and surrender can be forfeited and lost in flowery words that don't spring from the heart.

The modern Pharisee asks: Did I take my vitamins? Check. Did I feed the dog? Check. Did I take the trash out? Check. Did I have my quiet time? Check. And off he goes into his day, assured that everything is well with his soul because he had his "quiet time." If only he would wait before God, he might discover some things that would forever change his life.

Love Deeper than Words

Jesus wants you to experience His love to the fullest. The deepest expressions of love between a husband and wife aren't known through idle chatter. Sometimes the act of holding each other in silence speaks love most profoundly. That simple act may transcend words of love and convey its essence at the deepest levels.

Jesus Christ wants you to have more than cognitive knowledge of His love. He wants you to enjoy Him, to experience the fullness of His life within you. He wants to express Himself to you in such a way that you experience a supernatural chemistry that causes your relationship to be fulfilling for you both. He isn't simply the core of your religious beliefs. *He is your life.*

Brennan Manning expresses it well:

> The Christ within who is our hope of glory is not a matter of theological debate or philosophical speculation. He is not a hobby, a part-time project, a good theme for a book, or a last resort when all human effort fails. He is our life, the most real fact about us. He is the power and wisdom of God dwelling within us.[8]

Nine days before suffering a fatal heart attack, Thomas Kelly wrote the following words that describe well the spiritual neighborhood in which God calls us all to live:

> Life from the center is a life of unhurried peace and power. It is simple. It is serene. It is amazing. It is triumphant. It is radiant. It takes no time, but occupies all our time. And it makes our life programs new and overcoming. We need not get frantic. He

is at the helm. And when our little day is done we
lie down quietly in peace, for all is well.[9]

Any loving relationship is characterized by specific
moments of loving interaction. If you want to experience
the intimacy that your heavenly Father has for you, know
that His heart longs for you even more. His heart's desire
toward you burns with a single desire: "Allow Me to guide
you to a deeper level of intimacy with Me. I will hold you
continuously. I will fulfill the deepest desires of your soul
because I have placed them there. Come to me just as you
are and know without any doubt that you will be
accepted. You will be loved and nurtured. There is a
secret hideaway that I want to share with you. Come with
me—I want to whisper something to you, something you
will never forget."

Lord Jesus,
The thought of You inviting me to a secret place
where You will share Your love with me is overwhelming! I am amazed at such a thought, but I
do want to know You in that place. Teach me to
enter that place, to be still, to talk to You—even
without words at times. May Your heart and mine
beat as one. Hold me, Lord Jesus. With You, I am
safe.

G.R.A.C.E. GROUP QUESTIONS

1. How would you have explained the concept of meditation before reading this chapter? Has your understanding been changed in any way? If so, how? List three benefits of prayerful meditation.

2. Read the passage in John 4:20-24 and discuss what it means to worship "in spirit and in truth."

3. Identify other verses from the Bible about meditation that aren't mentioned in this chapter. What practical implications for believers today are found in those verses?

4. Describe what your own "prayer time" looks like. On a scale of 1-10, how satisfied are you with your prayer life? How has the Holy Spirit shown you that intimacy with God can be strengthened as you pray?

5. Discuss the concept of praying without words. How can this be done? What are the ways mentioned in this chapter that words can sometimes actually interfere with intimacy with God? What other ways might words hinder our pursuit for intimacy with Him?

10

Kiss Me Big

ANY EFFORT TO REDUCE THE LOVE OF GOD into words is an attempt destined to fail from the start. Those things which are infinite in scope can never be measured by finite tools. One would sooner successfully count the grains of sand on the beaches and in the oceans of the world than adequately enumerate the vastness of God's eternal love.

God loves you. The words have been spoken so many times by so many people that there is the danger that they have lost their edge, like a worn-out blade that no longer has the ability to cut. However, there is no alternate medium by which a book can communicate other than words. Don't come to the end of this book and allow the words to flow through your consciousness like a movie you watch and then forget as soon as you walk out of the theater.

Think about these words: *God loves me. Meditate* on them. Be transformed by them. Linger on each word, reflecting on its implication. Focus on each individual word until you *experience* its meaning. Allow the Living Water of divine affection to wash over you, healing you in the deepest recesses of your mind, your will, your emotions.

Don't rush past the words of this final chapter like an eager athlete pushing for the finish line. Read these pages *slowly*. If necessary, put the book down at points along the way and allow the Holy Spirit to forever seal your certainty about the passion of your Divine Lover Who will eternally be obsessed with you.

Know His love for you. *Feel* His affection toward you. Be embraced by Him and embrace Him in return. Fall into His arms and resolve to never leave again as long as you live. Sigh the sigh of relief that can only be known by those weary ones who, at last, have cast themselves unreservedly and with total abandon upon the eternal Resting Place. Inhale His peace, His tender acceptance, His gentle Presence. Revel in the oneness you share with Him. Bask in the realization, "God...loves...me."

GOD Loves Me

Do you understand the implications of the amazing truth that *God* loves you? Human love is volatile, unpredictable, and always subject to outside influence. Relationships can end through adverse circumstances or through death. Human relationships last only as long as there is one who is able and willing to give love and another who is able and willing to receive it.

The greatest love you will ever know from another human being is, at best, tentative. No loving relationship in this world lies beyond the reach of death. The terrain of human relationships can become a wasteland through the tragedy of terminal disease, bitter divorce, or even sheer boredom. Despite the promises of poetry and song, human love can wither and die.

Divine love exists in a category unto itself. The emotions that accompany human love may wax and wane, but

God promises, "I, the LORD, do not change" (Malachi 3:6). "For the LORD is good; His lovingkindness is everlasting And His faithfulness to all generations" (Psalm 100:5). God loves you, and He will never change His mind. His love for you isn't stronger at some times than it is at others. It is constant, without wavering.

On a summer day at the beach, people often enjoy being tanned by the ultraviolet rays of the sun. A common mistake many make is believing that they aren't as exposed to the effect of the sunlight during cloudy times as they are when the skies are completely sunny. It only takes one cloudy day at the beach to learn that whether the skies are cloudy or clear, the sun's effect isn't diminished. The sunlight cuts through clouds as if they weren't even there. Maybe the light can't be seen, but its ultraviolet rays are there in full force, at all times refusing to be squelched.

Nothing can shield you from the love of God. No clouds of discouragement, sin, doubts, negative feelings, trial and tribulation—nothing. *God* loves you. His love for you doesn't depend upon your spiritual consistency, dedication, or even your faith. Each of those are gifts from Him which develop as a *result* of His love for you. You neither give birth to them, nor maintain them. That's His business. Our role is to simply believe that we are loved by God regardless of our past or future track record.

Brennan Manning notes:

> Sometimes we harbor an unexpressed suspicion that he cannot handle all that goes on in our minds and hearts. We doubt that he can accept our hateful thoughts, cruel fantasies, and bizarre dreams. We wonder how he would deal with our primitive urges, our inflated illusions, and our exotic mental castles. The deep resistance to making ourselves so vulnerable, so naked, so totally unprotected is our

> implicit way of saying, "Jesus, I trust you, but there are limits."
>
> By refusing to share our fantasies, worries, joys, we limit God's lordship over life and make clear that there are parts of us that we do not wish to submit to a divine conversation.[1]

You may fall down, give up, turn your back, or just decide you've had enough of spiritual living. But the sun still shines on you, and nothing you do or don't do is going to change that fact. People may tire of our deficiencies, our irritating ways, and our self-centeredness, and they may give up on us. But *God* loves us, and He's not going to give up on us, no matter what.

Some years ago I became discouraged with God because of difficult circumstances I faced at the time. Ultimately, I turned my heart away from Him and, in a sense, walked away. For awhile, I went through the motions of ministry outwardly, but inwardly I was angry. I pouted. I fussed and fumed. I rebelled. After some time had passed, I came to my senses and recognized that when you're a Christian, there's nowhere else to go but to God.

One day I literally got on my knees and prayed, "Father, I'm sorry." Although this happened decades ago, I still remember clearly what happened. In my mind, I was turning around to come back to God. After all, I had left Him. However, when I turned around, He was there. It was as if I saw Him standing beside me. I came to realize that when I walked away, God came with me! When I saw Him through the eyes of faith, I then heard Him speak, "Are you finished (with your childish temper tantrum) yet? Good! Come here and let Me hug you!"

God loves us! How different His love is from that known by human beings! Irritable, whiny behavior won't do anything but cause Him to hug and comfort you. Even when we rebel and try to walk away from Him, He comes with us.

One day, after this experience with God, I paraphrased the Apostle Paul's words from Romans 8:38-39 to fit my own behavior:

> It's true! Nothing shall separate us from the love of God! For I am convinced that neither whining, nor pouting, nor unbelief, nor things we have done, nor things we are going to do, nor lack of spiritual consistency, nor failures of any kind shall be able to separate us from the love of God, which is in Christ Jesus our Lord!

Clouds may cover our perception of His divine passion, but with a love brighter than a thousand suns, He is "the Father of lights, with whom there is no variation or shifting shadow" (James 1:17). *God* loves you and He will never change. Never.

God LOVES Me

Catherine of Siena was a fourteenth-century Christian who wrote much about intimacy with God. She was once asked to describe the God of her journey. The brilliant, fiery Italian woman whispered in response, "He is crazed with love, drunk with love."[2] How would you describe the God of your own spiritual journey? Have you come to know Him primarily as the One who has revealed His *love* for you?

Todd expressed his own experience when he shared the following with me one day: "I believe *intellectually* that God loves me. After all, He is God. He *is* love. But although I know in my mind that He loves me, it doesn't do me a lot of good on a day-to-day basis. I'm trapped in poor personal habits. My marriage is shaky and, because of my busy work schedule, my children hardly know me.

I drag myself to church on Sunday, throw myself into the pew, and sit there thinking only one thing—tomorrow it all starts over again. What do I need to *do* to experience God's love in a meaningful way?"

The answer to his question rests in understanding that God's love isn't like any other love Todd has ever known. It's not like the *eros* of passionate love shared between a man and a woman being swept along by raging hormones. It's greater than the *phileo* brotherly love known by members of the same family. It far surpasses the *storge* love which suggests a warm relationship between two people who are completely familiar and comfortable with each other. Although these are certainly good, they are human types of love.

God's love is in a class of its own. It is *agape* love. It is divine in nature, needing no external catalyst to activate or perpetuate it. It isn't generated by some resident virtue in its recipient. It flows from an internal river known only to itself. It's a love that springs from the throne of God into this world through the fountainhead of Golgotha's cross.

It is a love that Todd and you and I did nothing to bring into existence. Therefore, because we did absolutely nothing to cause it, there is nothing we can do to stop it. It is a roaring river of raging passion rolling right over the righteous—those of us called by God.

We aren't to try to swim in the current, but just to yield to it and allow it to carry us wherever it will. Ironically enough, when we ultimately reach our downstream destination, we will find that we have been carried right back to the throne of God. In the meantime, the trip along the way is really just a *Jesus-journey* commonly known as "the Christian life."

How can we experience this outpouring of divine love in meaningful ways? We can't manage or manipulate its flow. We can only submit to it in what Robert Capon calls "the second rule of the life of grace." He explains:

Your part is just to make yourself available. Not to make anything happen. Not to achieve any particular intensity of subjective glow. Certainly not to work yourself up to some objective standard of performance that will finally con God into being gracious. Only to be *there*, and to be open to your Lover who without so much as a by-your-leave started this whole affair. And your attendance upon Him can include literally everything you do, because he has accepted it all in the Beloved: all good acts because they are vindicated in him; all rotten acts because they are reconciled in him; and even all religious acts because, in him, they have ceased to be transactions and become celebrations of something already accomplished.[3]

It is an immutable fact—God *loves* you. The divine love of our unchanging God will motivate Him for all eternity to lavish His goodness on you. There are no negotiations on your life and your future. The deal has been closed. You have been bought with a price and are at this very moment on your way home.

God loves ME

In 1981, the trial of Josephus Andersonan, an African American charged with the murder of a white policeman, took place in Mobile, Alabama. At the end of the trial the jury was unable to reach a verdict. The failure to reach a conviction stirred up members of the state chapter of the Ku Klux Klan. Two men decided that this wouldn't be the end of the matter.

On Saturday, March 21, 1981, Henry Hayes and James Knowles decided they would get revenge for the failure of the courts to convict Andersonan. They drove around Mobile in their car until they found 19-year-old Michael Donald walking home. Michael was a student and worked part time at the *Mobile Press Register*. After forcing him into the car, they beat Donald mercilessly with tree limbs, cut his throat, and then took him into the next county where they hung him by the neck until he was dead.

After a short investigation, both men were arrested, and in June of 1983, Knowles was found guilty and was sentenced to life in prison. Six months later, Henry Hayes was tried for murder, where he too was found guilty and sentenced to death. In a poignant moment at the close of his trial, Hayes turned to Michael's mother, Beulah Mae Donald and began to cry. "I can't bring your son back," he said. "God knows that if I could trade places with him, I would. But I can't."

In that situation, how would you respond to the person who had savagely murdered your teenaged child? Beulah Mae Donald's response brought the presence of Christ to the forefront in an Alabama county courtroom that day. With eyes brimming with tears, she quietly spoke these words to the man who had hung her son. "I already forgave you...from the day I found out who you all was. I asked God to take care of you, and He has." As she spoke, one reporter said there wasn't a dry eye in the courtroom. Beulah Mae Donald's forgiveness toward Henry Hayes melted the most hardened heart.

Like Henry Hayes, there is nothing any of us can do to reverse the sins we have committed. All have sinned against God (see Romans 3:23) and every person stands guilty before the cross of Jesus Christ. There aren't enough words or works by which we can undo our guilt. The element that makes grace so amazing is that the crucified Son of God, hanging from a Roman cross, beaten beyond recognition, bore the full consequence of your sin.

It's *your* guilt that served the wrath of God upon Jesus Christ until He had fully digested the bitter retribution for all your wrongdoing. It was for love of *you* that He remained there until He was engulfed by the eternal darkness of separation from God. He wanted *you* so badly that no price was too great to pay.

Do you remember the day when by faith you cried out in repentance, "I am so sorry! Please forgive me." On that day, the voice of Jesus gently spoke, "I already forgave you. From the day I first knew who you were, I asked my Father to take care of you, and now He has."

Because of the finished work of Jesus Christ, you can now relax. God loves *you* and has taken care of everything concerning you. Regrets about yesterday and fears about tomorrow vanish with the revelation that Christ is now your life, that "in Him [you now] live and move and exist" (Acts 17:28). Jesus Christ is the center and source of all things to you. Residing and resting in the realization of His love is your inheritance. You can now live out of His Life, the center of all things.

Allow this thought to incubate in your mind each day: "God loves *me*." Your relationship to Him isn't based on anything you have done or not done. Its basis is grounded in what *He* has done because of the great love He has for you.

"Why would God love *me?*" a new Christian wondered aloud to me one day.

"I have asked the same question about myself," I responded. It's a question every believer wonders about at times. God's decision to love you is hidden within the mystery of His providence and His infinite goodness. Perhaps we will never understand it, but we certainly can *believe* it and live our lives in light of that truth.

Do you really *believe* that God loves you? Perhaps the greatest breakthrough most Christians can ever experience is to accept God's acceptance. It's only when we're firmly grounded in the assurance of His unshakable love that we can really live freely. Until we understand the unconditional, irrevocable love of God for us, we will be doomed to a lifestyle focused on our own behavior. Your Divine Lover wants you to be focused on Him, not yourself.

How you progress through life will be determined in large part by how you view God's love for you. You can rest in Him and enjoy the journey, or you can anxiously struggle to stay in His good grace, a pointless and unnecessary endeavor. Robert Capon writes:

> Your life in grace is the life of a cripple on an escalator: as far as being able to walk upstairs is concerned, you are simply dead; there is nothing for *you* to do. But then you don't need to do anything, because the divine Floorwalker has kindly put you on the eternally moving staircase of Jesus—and up you go.
>
> What you do and think about yourself as you ascend will be delightful, or sad, or terrifying—depending. Delightful, insofar as you celebrate your free ride. Sad, insofar as you fight the escalator. Terrifying, insofar as you forget you're on it and go back to dwelling on your own inability to walk. But while all of that will matter to you, none of it will count against you. You're on your way. And all you have to do is believe it, and even the sadness and the terror become part of the ride up.
>
> And therefore the last rule of the life of grace is that nothing can separate you from it. Not your faults, not your vices, not your being a brat about refusing the cross—not even your rubbing salt in the wounds of Christ or kicking God when he is down. Because he took you by a voluntary crucifixion for your sake, and he takes it all as the price of taking you. Eventually you will cry about that, and those tears will be your repentance. But there isn't even

> any rush about that. He *knows he loves you*, and
> that's all that counts. You can catch up as you can.[4]

God loves you. It's so simple, yet so profound. Strangely enough, although God's love is the central message of the Bible, it's also the most difficult aspect of faith with which many Christians struggle. Trapped in the shallow waters of natural love, many simply cannot see the vast ocean of divine affection with its waves of *agape* billowing over them.

"But what if I were to turn my back on God and renounce Him? Surely you aren't suggesting that He would still love me!" "How can you believe that God could still love someone who committed *that* sin?" "Yes, God loves us, but you can take this *too far*. After all, what we do still matters to God!" "It's true that He is a God of love, *but He is also a God of wrath and justice!*"

Thus goes the litany of objections to divine love. Maybe you struggle with your own questions. Perhaps you can't reconcile certain things you believe to be true with this whole concept of a kind of divine love that is immeasurable, unconditional, and irrevocable.

I'm on the same side of the line as you are. There are aspects of God's love which I don't understand either. His love is too big for me to get my arms around and mentally manage. As hard as I've tried, I can't sort it all out. I still have unanswered questions about His love.

However, I have made a decision that continues to transform my life. I have chosen to *ap*prehend what I can't *com*prehend. I refuse to allow my limited ability to understand God's unlimited love to insulate me from enjoying it. Yes, there are still unresolved questions. Let the theologians figure them all out. Until they do, why not choose to believe in His love and receive it as something bigger and better than anything you've ever known?

John Eldredge offers a good example:

What is the truth of a kiss? Technically, in a modernistic sense, it is two sets of mandibles pressing together for a certain duration of time. Those of you who have experienced the wonder of a kiss will know that while true, this description is so untrue. It takes away everything beautiful and mysterious and passionate and intimate and leaves you with an icy cold fact. Those who know kissing feel robbed, those who don't are apt to say, "If that's what kissing is all about, I think I'd rather not."[5]

I can't imagine such a perspective in a human relationship. Like myself, many people travel extensively with their work. Can you imagine a person returning home from a business trip, and in anticipation of being with his mate, getting hung up on trying to understand the intellectual meaning of a kiss?

While there certainly are psychological and physiological factors associated with kissing, that is the farthest thing from *my* mind when I come home to Melanie. Tennessee Ernie Ford summed up the basic elements of such a moment in his old song, *Kiss Me Big*. No talk from him about "mandibles contacting each other for a certain duration of time." His assessment was both simple and practical: "Pull down the shades. Unhook the phone. Pucker up, baby. Daddy's comin' home!"

That attitude expresses the heart of Jesus toward you. He wants your relationship with Him to thrill you. You are His bride and He is head over heels in love with you. He plans to spend eternity proving His love to you in ways beyond your wildest dreams. His love is pure, yet passionate. It is an objective fact with profound subjective implications for your life. He longs for you to know how much He loves you, to *feel* how much He loves you, to *see* how much He loves you.

Some will be quick to caution against the dangers of shallow emotionalism. Indeed, there is a legitimate risk that some will reduce their understanding of the relationship they have to Christ to the place of emotionalism. Few would deny that, *but* there is an equal or perhaps even greater risk that many will spend their lives relating to Christ exclusively through their intellect.

The deepest human relationships of our lives permeate our mind, our emotions, and our choices. Our relationship to Christ is no different. He is not just a propositional truth to be learned, nor a mystical feeling to be experienced. He is greater than all of that.

He is the Father who falls on the neck of returning prodigals and with tears of joy streaming down His cheeks, kisses them and shouts with laughter, "My son is home! Let's have a party" (see Luke 15:20-24). He is the Mother who smothers Her babies in kisses as they snuggle against her breasts (see Psalm 131:2). He is the Lover who says, "I love you *so much* that I'll kiss you right out in public, and I don't care who sees me! In fact, nobody would blame me!" (see Song of Solomon 8:1). He is the Artist who points to you and declares proudly to the universe, "Look what I made!" (see Ephesians 2:10). He is the Composer who sings love songs to you! (see Zephaniah 3:17). He is the Wealthy Merchant who sold everything He had so that He could make you His own (see Matthew 13:45-46). He is the King of kings and Lord of lords who left the glory of His exalted throne in heaven, waded through the filth of this sinful world, and descended into the horrors of hell—all for one simple reason. He looked beyond the horror and saw you standing on the other side, waiting for Him to rescue you.

With the kiss of grace He awakened you from your sleep of spiritual death. He swept you off your feet and is now carrying you toward the eternal honeymoon home He has prepared for you (see John 14:2-3). Having already conquered death and hell, nothing stands in His way. Nothing will deter Him from His mission.

The marriage feast has been prepared. The table has been set. You stand in the corridor of time at the place where the door of eternity is about to swing open to receive you. Just beyond the door is singing. It is a great multitude of wedding guests who have anxiously awaited your arrival. As you soon step across the boundary from time into eternity, you will hear their song:

> Hallelujah! For the Lord our God, the Almighty reigns! Let us rejoice and be glad and give the glory to Him, for the marriage of the Lamb has come and His bride has made herself ready (Revelation 19:6-7).

In that moment, all the cares of the earth-life will have disappeared. You will turn, look into the eyes of the One who set His heart on you an eternity ago. He will look deeply into your eyes with a penetrating gaze and gently whisper your name. With a heart flooded by His love, you can only speak a single word. But that one word will embody the essence of all that exists in time and eternity. With tears of joy and a realization that everything is complete, you will simply whisper, "Jesus...*oh Jesus!*"

Dear Father,
I eagerly await that day when this earth-life will be over and I see You face-to-face. Your love for me overwhelms me. You really do love me more than I could ever imagine! May I grow in my understanding of Your love. You are precious to me. I give myself completely to You from this point and throughout eternity. I do love You so much.

G.R.A.C.E. Group Questions

1. In one paragraph, write what you believe God would write if He were to send a personalized love note to you.

2. Identify three Bible verses which speak of God's lovingkindness and patience. Paraphrase the verses in your own words.

3. Read the story of the prodigal son in Luke 15 and name three comparisons between the love of the father in the story and the love God has for you.

4. When Jesus Christ comes to take you home to your eternal honeymoon home, what is the first question you will ask Him?

5. Read Romans 8:38-39. Paraphrase the verse to reflect the history of your own life experiences.

Notes

1—Too Busy for Love

1. Becky Freeman, "Marriage 911," *Home Life*, Dec. 2000, p. 37.
2. Thomas R. Kelly, *A Testament of Devotion* (San Francisco: Harper & Brothers, 1941), p. 9.
3. Ibid., p. 3

2—Forgiven and Forgotten

1. Lauren F. Winner, "Evangelist to Soul Friend," *Christianity Today*, Oct. 2, 2000.
2. I have given a more complete explanation of God, time, and forgiveness in chapter 10 of my book *Grace Land* (Eugene, OR: Harvest House Publishers, 2001).
3. Brennan Manning, *Ruthless Trust* (San Francisco: HarperSanFrancisco, 2000), p. 155.
4. From "Known" by Dr. Charles K. Robinson, quoted in M. Scott Peck, *People of the Lie* (New York: Simon and Schuster, 1983), pp. 267-68.

5—The Silenced Cry

1. Brennan Manning, *Abba's Child: The Cry of the Heart for Intimate Belonging* (Colorado Springs: NavPress, 1994), p. 30.
2. *Easton's Revised Bible Dictionary*, from The Online Bible (Winterbourne, Ontario, Canada: Timnathserah, Inc., 1987).
3. My book *Grace Rules*, chapter 8 titled "A Smiling God" may help you develop a more complete concept of God and His love.

6—*The Dance of Grace*

1. *The Wycliffe Bible Commentary* (Chicago: Moody Press, 1962). Wycliffe's commentary suggests, "On Hittite bestiality, consult G.A. Barton, *Archaeology and the Bible*, pp. 423-426. Ezekiel was stressing the heathenism in Israel's background."
2. Song of Solomon 1:15; 2:13; 4:1,7,9; 7:6.
3. Brent Curtis and John Eldredge, *The Sacred Romance* (Nashville: Thomas Nelson Publishers, 1997), p. 97.
4. For a printed copy of Cheryl Buchanan's complete story, contact our office at 1-800-472-2311.
5. Song of Solomon 2:10-13.

7—*From Must to Trust*

1. Jeff Imbach, *The River Within* (Colorado Springs: NavPress), 1998, p. 262.
2. The Old Testament says that Adam *knew* Eve, and she bore him a son. The New Testament says that Mary did not *know* a man until after Jesus was born. Both references evidence the fact that the word *know* sometimes denotes an intimacy far beyond the casual meaning often associated with the word in contemporary culture.
3. Thomas R Kelly, *A Testament of Devotion* (San Francisco: Harper & Brothers, 1941), pp. vii-viii. From Richard Foster's introduction.
4. Ibid., p. 45.

8—*The Fire Burned*

1. Thomas R. Kelly, *A Testament of Devotion* (San Francisco: Harper & Brothers, 1941), p. 120.
2. John Eldredge, *The Journey of Desire* (Nashville: Thomas Nelson Publishers, 2000), pp. 137-38.
3. Ibid., pp. 204-05.
4. Jeff Imbach, *The River Within* (Colorado Springs: NavPress, 1998), p. 98.
5. *Grace Walk*, *Grace Rules*, and *Grace Land* (Eugene, OR: Harvest House Publishers).
6. Henri Nouwen, *The Way of the Heart* (San Francisco: Harper Collins Publishers, 1981), p. 45.
7. Grace Walk Mexico is the office through which we are reaching into Latin America to share God's grace. For more information on our international ministries or other aspects of Grace Walk Ministries, please write us at the address provided at the back of this book or visit our web site at www.gracewalk.org.

8. Gordon MacDonald, *Ordering Your Private World* (Nashville: Thomas Nelson Publishers, 1984), p. 126.

9. Kelly, *A Testament of Devotion*, p. 46.

10. Lauren F. Winner, "Evangelist to Soul Friend," *Christianity Today*, Oct. 2, 2000.

11. Kelly, *A Testament of Devotion*, p. 84.

9—*The Holy Hideaway*

1. Buck Anderson, "Kindred Spirit," Dallas Theological Seminary, Winter 1994, pp. 11-12.

2. Ibid.

3. Jean-Nicholas Grou (1730–1803), *How to Pray*. Grou lived in France and Holland. After having his life transformed in 1767 while attending a spiritual retreat, he spent much of his life writing and speaking on the subject of spiritual growth, particularly the practice of prayer.

4. Thomas R. Kelly, *A Testament of Devotion* (San Francisco: Harper & Brothers, 1941), p. 118.

5. Ibid., p. 93.

6. Grou, *How to Pray*.

7. Ibid.

8. Brennan Manning, *Abba's Child* (Colorado Springs: NavPress, 1994), p. 151.

9. Kelly, *A Testament of Devotion*, p.100.

10—*Kiss Me Big*

1. Brennan Manning, *Ruthless Trust* (San Francisco: HarperSanFrancisco, 2000), pp. 117-18.

2. Ibid., p. 69.

3. Robert Farrar Capon, *Between Noon and Three* (Grand Rapids, MI: William B. Eerdmans Publishing Company), 1997, p. 293.

4. Capon, *Between Noon and Three*, pp. 293-94.

5. John Eldredge, *The Journey of Desire* (Nashville: Thomas Nelson Publishers, 2000), p. 203.

Bibliography

Anderson, Neil, and Mike & Julia Quarles. *Freedom from Addiction.* Ventura, CA: Regal Books, 1996.

Brother Lawrence. *The Practice of the Presence of God.* Grand Rapids, MI: Fleming H. Revell, 1967.

Capon, Robert Farrar. *Between Noon and Three.* Grand Rapids, MI: William B. Eerdmans Publishing Company, 1997.

Chambers, Oswald. *Conformed to His Image.* Fort Washington, PA: Christian Literature Crusade, 1996.

Edman, Raymond V. *They Found the Secret.* Grand Rapids, MI: Zondervan Publishing House, 1960.

Eldredge, John. *The Journey of Desire.* Nashville, TN: Thomas Nelson Publishers, 2000.

———. *Wild at Heart.* Nashville, TN: Thomas Nelson Publishers, 2001.

George, Bob. *Classic Christianity.* Eugene, OR: Harvest House Publishers, 1987.

———.*Growing in Grace.* Eugene, OR: Harvest House Publishers, 1991.

Gillham, Anabel. *The Confident Woman.* Eugene, OR: Harvest House Publishers, 1993.

Gillham, Bill. *Lifetime Guarantee.* Eugene, OR: Harvest House Publishers, 1987.

———. *What God Wishes Christians Knew About Christianity*. Eugene, OR: Harvest House Publishers, 1998.

Gillham, Preston. *Things Only Men Know*. Eugene, OR: Harvest House Publishers, 1999.

Hession, Roy. *The Calvary Road*. Fort Washington, PA: Christian Literature Crusade, 1997.

Huegel, F.J. *Bone of His Bone*. Fort Washington, PA: Christian Literature Crusade, 1994.

Imbach, Jeff. *The River Within*. Colorado Springs: NavPress, 1998.

Kelly, Thomas R. *A Testament of Devotion*. San Francisco: HarperSanFrancisco, 1996.

MacDonald, Gordon. *Ordering Your Private World*. Nashville, TN: Thomas Nelson Publishers, 1984.

Manning, Brennan. *Abba's Child*. Colorado Springs: NavPress, 1994.

———. *Ruthless Trust*. San Francisco: HarperSanFrancisco, 2000.

———. *The Ragamuffin Gospel*. Sisters, OR: Multnomah Publishers, 1990.

Maxwell, L.E. *Born Crucified*. Chicago: Moody Press, 1945.

McVey, Steve. *Grace Walk*. Eugene, OR: Harvest House Publishers, 1995.

———. *Grace Rules*. Eugene, OR: Harvest House Publishers, 1998.

———. *Grace Land*. Eugene, OR: Harvest House Publishers, 2000.

Murray, Andrew. *Abide in Christ*. Fort Washington, PA: Christian Literature Crusade, 1992.

———. *The Believer's Secret of Obedience*. Bloomington, MN: Bethany House Publishing, 1982.

Nee, Watchman. *The Normal Christian Life*. Wheaton, IL: Tyndale House Publishers, 1977.

Needham, David. *Alive for the First Time*. Sisters, OR: Multnomah Publishers, 1995.

Nouwen, Henri. *The Way of the Heart*. San Francisco: Harper Collins Publishers, 1991.

Penn-Lewis, Jessie. *War on the Saints*. New Kensington, PA: Whitaker House, 1997.

Piper, John. *Desiring God*. Sisters, OR: Multnomah Publishers, 1986.

————. *The Legacy of Sovereign Joy*. Wheaton, IL: Crossway Books, 2000.

Redpath, Alan. *Victorious Christian Living*. Grand Rapids, MI: Fleming H. Revell Company, 1955.

Smith, Hannah Whitall. *The God of All Comfort*. Chicago: Moody Press, 1956.

Stone, Dan, and Greg Smith. *The Rest of the Gospel*. One Press, 2000.

Thomas, Ian. *The Saving Life of Christ / The Mystery of Godliness*. Grand Rapids, MI: Zondervan Publishers, 1988.

Trumbull, Charles G. *Victory in Christ*. Fort Washington, PA: Christian Literature Crusade, 1959.

The Song of
Divine Invitation
by
Cheryl Buchanan

In a room filled with darkness and people in despair
I sit in filth with clothes of rags, without a will to care.
Then a Man dressed in scarlet walks into the room;
The air that once was stale and cold is filled with sweet perfume.
His eyes are filled with searching, among faces pale and ashen;
He makes His way among us with a heart compelled by passion.
Then suddenly His eyes meet mine, my heart begins to race,
I find myself longing to feel His warm embrace.

He stops and stands before me as if He has found a prized possession.
His eyes are tender, filled with joy, with sweet and calm compassion.
With gentleness He takes my cheek within His soothing hand;
He turns my face towards His, I feel I know this Man.
His tender gaze pierces through the darkness of my soul,
I feel He knows all about me, every secret that I hold.
With a voice like a whisper that sounds just like a song,
He speaks the words of love for which my heart has longed.
"Come dance with Me, My darling, Come dance with Me, My love;
Come dance, My bride, My chosen one, Come dance with Me above."

As I rise from my darkness, the room is filled with light,
And as we dance, His robe is turned from scarlet into white.
He holds me close and tenderly within His warm embrace,
Somehow I know He loves me and know that I am safe.
All around me I hear music that reaches deep within my soul,
My spirit feels alive—reborn with joy—for now I'm whole.
We slowly dance around the room as He holds me to his side,
With gentleness and tenderness, He tells me I'm *His* bride.

And as we dance He sings a song that fills my eyes with tears,
Of love that heals a hardened heart and quiets every fear.
He tells me I'm His treasure, I'm His joy and His reward,
His unique beloved creation, the one He loves and He adores.
His song is like a poem that He is singing just to me,
His face is filled with joy; it sets my spirit free.

Then gently He leans over and places a kiss upon my cheek,
And with words that fill my heart with gladness, He softly begins to speak.
He tells me of a gift that's been made especially for me,
Woven by loving passion, it will clothe, set me free.
As we stop He takes a hold on both my outstretched hands,
He then speaks with boldness, and to the host of heaven commands:

"Bring Me her silk garments, bracelets and golden crown.
Bring Me her leather sandals and white embroidered gown,
Bring Me the necklaces, the earrings and the wine,
Bring the oil that I will use to cleanse and make her Mine.
For this is *My* bride, My chosen one who brings My heart delight,
This is the one I died for, My beloved beautiful bride."

And instantly my garments are changed from rags to robes,
For He has dressed me in His splendor, for all of heaven to behold.
As He stands in front of me, joy beams across His face,
For today He has made me holy, pure, and filled with grace.
He takes my hand, pulls me close and gently sings to me,
Of how this dance of love will last through all eternity.
Of how I am His holy, pure, and beautiful creation,
And once again He sings the song of divine invitation.

"Come dance with Me, My darling, Come dance with Me, My love,
You are My bride, My chosen one, Come dance with Me above.
I've paid the price to have you, to hold you to My side,
My joy, My one, My only, beloved, beautiful bride."

A Personal Word

If your life has been influenced by reading *A Divine Invitation,* I would be happy to hear from you. The purpose of Grace Walk Ministries is to share the liberating message of the believer's identity in Christ through teaching and preaching, radio, television, books, tapes, and mission outreaches. For a complete list of available resources, please contact me at the following address. I also invite you to visit our web site at www.gracewalk.org.

Dr. Steve McVey
Grace Walk Ministries
P.O. Box 725368
Atlanta, GA 31139-9368
800-472-2311
Email: gracewalk@aol.com

May God continue to bless you in your own grace walk as you come to "know Him, and the power of His resurrection and the fellowship of His sufferings" (Philippians 3:10).

Other Steve McVey books available from Harvest House Publishers

GRACE WALK

What you've always wanted in the Christian life...but never expected. Learn to push self-sufficiency aside and let Christ live through you. Experience the grace walk, and know the spiritual fulfillment you have been striving for all along.

Trade Paper (192 pp.), **1-56507-3215**

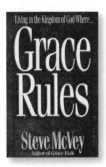

GRACE RULES

Understanding the concepts of law and grace can help Christians live out their identity in Christ. By discovering how Jesus' grace can consistently flow out of our lives, believers can experience a satisfying and abundant Christian life.

Trade Paper (208 pp.), **1-56507-8977**

GRACE AMAZING

(formerly *Grace Land*)

McVey shows that, through God's amazing grace, Christians have every spiritual blessing in Christ; they have true rest in Jesus; and the Father is in love with them because He's in love with His Son.

Trade Paper (192 pp.), **0-7369-1177-4**

Available March 2004